Kingdom Come in Everyday Speech

Don Cupitt

Kingdom Come in Everyday Speech

SCM PRESS

0 334 02799 3

This edition first published 2000
by SCM Press
9–17 St Albans Place, London N1 0NX

SCM Press is a division of
SCM-Canterbury Press Ltd

Printed in Great Britain by
Biddles Ltd, Guildford and King's Lynn

For the members of
Sea of Faith

Contents

Introduction

This book is the third and probably the last of the 'Everyday Speech' books, in which I have been trying to open up a new field of religious enquiry. It may be called 'ordinary-language theology'. The aim is to demonstrate what religious ideas are currently embedded in and expressed by our ordinary language. In our post-metaphysical age few people think that the traditional 'natural' or 'rational' theology can deliver anything, so in order to replace it I am proposing ordinary-language theology as a descriptive study of the common religious philosophy that is built into everyday speech and thereby belongs to us all.

Ordinary-language philosophy was prominent in Britain for a short period after the Second World War, the leading practitioners being Wittgenstein, Gilbert Ryle and J. L. Austin. Wittgenstein in particular introduced the idea that there is nothing deeper than ordinary language. It already presupposes – it already has built into it – our basic communally-evolved sense of ourselves, our lives, our world, our knowledge, and time and space. This led me to the parallel thought that there isn't, and there can't be, anything deeper than or prior to the basic religious philosophy of life that we have gradually evolved amongst ourselves, and now possess coded into our language in compressed form.

Educated people tend to assume that ordinary language, if it has any philosophical or religious ideas built into it at all, must surely teach naïve realism. Or perhaps Cartesianism, with its sharp contrast between the material and mental realms. The contribution of Ryle and Austin was to suggest, on the contrary, that ordinary language is philosophically sharp. Austin, for example, drew attention to the distinctions in ordinary language between just *listening* or *looking*, and actually *hearing* or *seeing* something; and this observation shows us that in ordinary language perception is already recognized as being an interpretative and constructive *activity*: out of raw sense data we build the world we see. Ryle, too, in his great book *The Concept of Mind* made highly effective use of idioms from ordinary language in support of a view of 'the mind' – roughly, as a collection of capacities – which seemed outrageous at the time but is commonplace now.

The discovery that ordinary language can be philosophically very sharp, and is often well ahead of its users, has been highly stimulating to me. Over the years, as I have struggled to express new ideas, I have repeatedly found that I have got there rather late, because *ordinary language says it already*, and says it as pithily as one could ever hope to say it oneself. Ordinary language, for example, is highly perspectivist: **That's the way you see it, but it's not the way I see it.** Ordinary language already knows all about anti-realism: **Life's what you make it**, it says. Ordinary language is the best radical theologian, for it has already largely reinterpreted religion in purely this-worldly terms. And as I have more and more come to see all this, I have naturally been tickled by its dialectical possibilities: I can answer all my orthodox critics by showing them that they themselves already hold the views that they denounce in me. Ordinary language is bigger than all of us put together: its terse and forceful idioms incorporate our deepest-available sense of how things are with us human beings. And nobody can really drop out of it, because we are always within it and always presuppose it.

We differ somewhat, however, from the people of the Wittgenstein/Ryle/Austin generation, because we are much more historically-minded. Ordinary language is no sort of absolute and cannot be made into a new 'foundation' for all thought and knowledge, because it changes quite quickly – and certainly, a lot more quickly than was recognized fifty years ago. We seem to be living in a time of rapid deep change. That is why, when I say that philosophy and theology begin within and grow out of ordinary language, I am not making ordinary language into a new stable and unchanging matrix or foundation for all knowledge. I am rather saying that we need to study ordinary language in order to learn which way the wind is blowing, and how the foundations are shifting.

A time of rapid deep change is a time when one must be continually questioning, reviewing, and perhaps changing one's own deep assumptions. One keeps on having to go back to the beginning and start again – which explains why there are certain subject-areas in which it is inappropriate to look for evidence of historical progress. They include philosophy, religion, ethics, art, and literary and social theory. These areas of enquiry are permanently disputatious, self-questioning and somewhat politicized. It cannot be helped. In other areas such as bridge-building or chemistry we can over the years accumulate and transmit skills and algorithms. There is progress, and we can be said to stand on the shoulders of our predecessors. But in the earlier-mentioned group of topics – religion, philosophy, ethics, art and 'critical theory' – in these areas, talk of progress is out of place. Each generation needs in principle to be capable of checking what is happening to the current deep assumptions, and making a fresh start.

This does not mean that one can afford to neglect the great figures of the past. On the contrary, it is not possible to be a good revolutionary unless one is first steeped in the tradition. In my present terms this means simply that, *after* first attending to what has been done in the past, one then needs also to attend closely to what is currently happening in ordinary language in order to find out which way the wind is blowing *today*.

In *The Meaning of It All . . .*, I introduced the idea that ordinary language posits and aspires after a 'kingdom-world' – a purely human, moral world like the kingdom of God in the Bible, or Kant's kingdom of ends. Language developed for the sake of human networking, which in my family at least is feminist for gossip on the telephone. (Not that there is anything wrong with gossip, for as was pointed out in *The Meaning of It All*, p.68, 'gossip' is *God sib*, and is a highly theological term.)

Ordinary language therefore looks for a world of unfettered and mutually transparent human communication, in which everything non-human that encircles us and threatens us – **it all** – is either chained up or at least deferred or kept at bay. Language's own philosophy is a form of radical humanism, and its politics is democratic. Reality is or should be made a network of persons whose impersonal environment sustains, but does not distort, their free converse with each other.

The present little book takes that theme a step further by asking how far in ordinary language today the traditional religious eschatology has been 'realized', or made actual in the present age. If indeed ordinary language has brought heaven and hell forward, so that they have become states of affairs or states of mind that are readily accessible to people now, what are the implications? Are we already living in post-history, in the world at the end of the world that has no further world lying beyond it? The answer seems to be Yes: ordinary language's basic cosmological distinction is no longer that between God and the created order, including Man, but that between the human world and the encircling non-human. Ordinary language seems to picture Christianity as having already moved into its post-ecclesiastical and final stage of development. In which case ordinary language is not just some generations or centuries ahead of the church and its ways of thinking, but a whole religious epoch or dispensation ahead.

In our end is our beginning: we should not be surprised to find ordinary language turning out to be so avant-garde theologically. It *evolved* as the human communication system, so it naturally tends to build a world that is a human communications network, and it naturally seeks to get rid of or filter out background noise and whatever else threatens to corrupt or distort the messages. Thus at the end of writing these three short books I have been startled by something obvious: *of course* ordinary language presupposes kingdom theology. It must, obviously.

Then why did the church get stuck in a time-warp? It forgot the dialectical interplay between church theology and kingdom theology which is an essential structural feature of Christianity.

Through the belief in its own indefectibility the church fell into a kind of idolatry of itself and its own doctrine-system. An old, sad story; and the difficult situation of the contemporary church is compounded by the fact that its own kingdom-theology tradition has become secularized and has grown away from it to form our modern democratic politics, our traditions of radical dissent, our highly multi-ethnic and even *Pentecostal* modern states, and our humanitarianism, belief in human rights and expressionist art and spirituality. In short, our postmodern secular culture is not *opposed* to Christianity, but rather should be regarded as hinting at, or even as just *being*, Christianity's own next stage of historical development. Hence the uncomfortable and paradoxical situation of Christianity today: the church, authoritarian, hierarchical and unreformed, coexists uneasily with a secular version of its own future which is morally much superior to it in all matters to do with freedom of thought, democracy, human rights and sexual ethics. The embarrassing gap here can be narrowed only by persuading the church to start taking an interest in kingdom theology.

The long dominance of ecclesiastical theology still leads many people to see Christianity as a religion of other-worldly individual salvation. But kingdom theology, rooted in the hopes of the Israelite prophets and in the tradition of Jesus' teaching, is communal, this-worldly and utopian. It sees religion as being about, not just *my* personal salvation, but the moral quality of *our* social life. The kingdom world is an egalitarian world, multi-ethnic, globalized and humanitarian, in which people are liberated from poverty and toil, from all structures of religious and political oppression, and from ethnic antagonism and the darkness of false consciousness. Religious hope and longing for such a world is very strong in the texts of the Hebrew prophets, but ecclesiastical theology looked to these texts with one interest in mind only – the confirmation of its own dogmas – and so lost their larger message. The teaching of Jesus was similarly lost as the church concentrated all its attention upon its doctrines of his person and his atoning work. At the Enlightenment the old utopian religious hopes were revived, but in predominantly secular forms – anarchism, socialism, the belief in progress – and the church has not yet been able to recognize or try to come to terms with its own older, better half.

I have added two appendices to the main argument. The first tries to develop and clarify the distinction between ecclesiastical theology and kingdom theology, and the second is about the extent to which almost all thought in the old, pre-Enlightenment Western tradition depended upon a very high valuation of unequal relationships. Inequalities, often first created by force, were the building blocks with which reality was constructed.

Kingdom theology, along with its many offshoots such as socialism, anarchism and every sort of utopianism, has always dreamt of a world of equals. An amusing naif illustration of this is the old Christian iconography of heaven, in which everybody looked rather alike, dressed rather alike, and was the same height. It was a world seemingly made of human persons only, in a peaceable garden setting, or in a choir or orchestra. And did you know that everybody in heaven was thirty-three years old, that being the age of the resurrection body; the perfect age, the age of Christ at his own death and resurrection? It is a curious feature of classical Christianity that it combined a world-view built entirely out of inequalities with extreme egalitarianism in its picture of heaven.

I attempted a postmodern theology in four books in the late 1980s. They were *Life Lines*, 1986; *The Long-Legged Fly*, 1987; *The New Christian Ethics*, 1988; and *Radicals and the Future of the Church*, 1989. Making a fresh attempt at a postmodern theology in these three little Everyday Speech books, I hope that I now have a better (because more empirically-based) method and a clearer, more systematic result. Given the present very low condition of academic theology in Britain and elsewhere, it seems to me important that someone should try to give the subject a rational, empirical method that delivers results of genuine interest to ordinary people.

As in the earlier books in this series, **bold** type is used for the words and idioms from everyday speech to which I am drawing attention. Familiar quotations that are themselves also part of everyday speech are printed in *italics*.

I find belatedly that the title *The Meaning of It All* has been used already, for a posthumous collection of essays by the physicist Richard Feynman (US ed., Addison-Wesley Longman Inc. 1998; UK ed., Penguin Books, 1999). But Feynman's approach is very different from mine.

Thanks to Hugh Rayment-Pickard, Steven Shakespeare, Petra Green and Linda Allen. This book is for my many friends in Sea of Faith.

D.C.

I

Sheer Bliss

How does it come about that our late-modern or postmodern age is so highly secular, whilst at the same time seeing itself as a time of religious fulfilment? Why is postmodernity *both* cynically nihilistic *and* obsessively theological? The Death of God is now widely recognized to have occurred and traditional forms of religion are everywhere in steep decline, yet the old vocabulary and symbolism of religion are more than ever ubiquitous in popular speech and popular cultural display. When we go on **holiday**, it has to be to a tourist **paradise** where we can get **blissed out**: it's **absolute heaven**. Advertising in particular bombards us with seductive imagery derived from religion, imagery promising that ideal beauty and happiness can be realized on earth and in this present life – in childhood, in domestic life, in our holidays, and in our sensuous experience. Our consumer culture actually *works* by continually promising us the Earthly Paradise.

Amongst the group of words involved here, **heaven** turns out to be much the most prolific generator of new idioms and the metaphor most often used. Both it and **hell** are seen in this-worldly terms. Similarly, **paradise** tends to be associated with landscaped gardens and with the tropics and strong colours, **Eden** with memories of childhood, and **bliss** with the sensuous happiness of women. It is to be noted that, although heaven is still 'above', all four words are nowadays used chiefly or entirely in connection with *this* world. Only when we are talking to young children do we still say that a dead person has 'gone to heaven'. Otherwise, **heaven** is simply the sky above us, or it is a state of affairs or a state of consciousness that is readily accessible to us in this life: it is always *there*, waiting for us, offering itself to us:

absolute heaven
sheer heaven
heaven on earth
all this and heaven too
God in heaven / God's in his heaven
the kingdom of heaven
heaven lies about us in our infancy
a marriage made in heaven
to be young was very heaven
it stinks to high heaven
good heavens!
heavens above! / for heaven's sake!
the seventh heaven
manna from heaven
heaven-sent
Heaven, I'm in heaven (song title)
Heaven's Gate (film title)
heaven knows!
raising one's eyes to heaven (in mock-exasperation)
heaven dust (heroin, cocaine)
heavenly (compare **divine, godlike**)
the heaven-born (senior members of the ICS)
the heavens open (**the heavens** = the sky)
move heaven and earth to do something

Hell is complicated by the sheer number of slang expressions in which it figures, but it too is nowadays seen as a this-worldly state of affairs. It may be a slum, or a state of excessive and stressful noise, speed and disorder, or a subjective state of extreme unhappiness. Examples follow:

hell's kitchen (a New York slum)
hell on earth

all hell broke loose (pandemonium: compare
merry hell, play hell, hellzapoppin, hell for leather, hell's bells, like a bat out of hell, hell on wheels)
neighbours from hell / the job from hell
go to hell
the hell of depression, a **private hell**
I've been through hell
hell is other people (Sartre, *Huis Clos* Sc. V)
hell is oneself (T. S. Eliot)

Surveying some two or three hundred idioms, I find only three with traditional theological content:

not a hope in hell
hell-bent (= perhaps reprobate, predestined to damnation)
I hope he rots in hell

Although the words are in frequent use, **paradise** and **Eden** supply only a few idioms:

England is the paradise of women
the earthly paradise
paradise fish/flycatcher/kingfisher/birds of

One foot in Eden still I stand . . .
This other Eden . . .
the garden of Eden / *New Eden* (gardening magazine)
the Vale of Eden (Cumbria, England: compare **Arcadia**)

bliss, blissful, bliss out, blissout (a state of ecstasy)
Bliss was it in that dawn to be alive
wedded bliss
blissful ignorance / *where ignorance is bliss, 'tis folly to be wise*
unadulterated bliss, sheer bliss, pure bliss
a sigh of bliss

As well as its strong association with the tropics and palm-fringed beaches, paradise is also a beloved place and a private garden. We have, quite recently, thoroughly democratized the earthly paradise. Once, only princes lived in houses set in ornamental pleasure-gardens.[1] Like the dead at Agra in India, they inhabited a garden-world that was expressly designed to be a framed image of **heaven on earth**, a *claustrum* (close, cloister or enclosure), secluded and exclusive. But when we built the first garden suburbs (and, later, the garden cities) we democratized the dream: *everybody's* house was to be a castle and a *sanctum*, surrounded by a private garden. Look at the mantelpiece over the hearth in the main living-room. It has long been the custom to furnish it like an altar, but with one major difference: there is a clock where the cross might be, because this domestic sanctuary is in the public and common temporal world.

It doesn't seem to worry us that our heaven is sensual and temporal: **chocolate heaven**, we say, **smiling beatifically** (**coffee heaven** is often seen, and sometimes one even hears of **petrol heaven** – fuel economy). We are very keen to keep up the old vocabulary, even in cases where it is wildly at odds with modern science. When it suddenly starts to rain heavily, we declare that **the heavens have opened**, in spite of the fact that it is many centuries since any of us really thought that the sky is an upside-down glass colander through whose holes, 'the windows of heaven',[2] God pours down the rain upon us. We still insist that something **stinks to high heaven**, as if God up there may get wind of it just as he does in the book of Genesis,[3] though one may wonder whether even Evangelicals really think that God sits sniffing in the sky overhead.

We love the old language of **heaven, hell, paradise, Eden, bliss** and **beatitude**, and even seem to insist that we are using it 'literally', for when we say **sheer heaven** or **absolute heaven** we mean **pure** or **unadulterated** heaven. It is as if the whole supernatural world of religion has in very recent times been comprehensively brought forward into the present age: **heaven on earth**. In postmodernity *most of our experience* has a religious flavour, heavenly, hellish, or purgatorial. And the airport? – It's Limbo, an intermediate world in which people drift about, waiting to be taken away to a better place.

There are other more striking examples of the realization of eschatology in present sensuous experience. Aldous Huxley's *The Doors of Perception, and Heaven and Hell* (Penguin 1959) was an influential pioneer work of our postmodern drug culture; and a friend points out to me that 'descriptions of sexual orgasm do have an eschatological flavour: coming, climaxing, *the earth moves* and so on'. He's right: they do. *Le petit mort* is another scrap of evidence.

It seems that we positively *expect* **heaven on earth**. One reason for this must be that the older eschatology never had, and could not have, a proper descriptive language of its own. Nobody was in a position to say what the joys of heaven would be, and the ancient writers had therefore to resort to earthly metaphors that made heaven sound like El Dorado, or a king's palace: a city of gold and jewels, sweeter than honey, perfect music, beautiful gardens, the absence of suffering, endless light and love. As a result, heaven has always sounded like an improved experience of the ordinary world – **the best things in life**. For us postmoderns the difference is that heaven now actually *is* an improved experience of the ordinary world. Heaven has come down to earth, in the sense that our much greater wealth has enabled millions of us to enjoy in this life pleasures that our forebears could only dream of enjoying after death.

Evidently some radical secularization has taken place here. How has it come about?

Our earlier enquiries suggested that the event has taken place in two stages. First, the French Revolution marked the end, not only of the *ancien régime*, but of the old fixed and ready-made cosmos-out-there. Beginning with the philosophy of Kant, a new radical-humanist world-view began to appear, in which people began to recognize that they have not been inserted into a ready-made working system of things with built-in laws, but rather that they themselves have very gradually over the millennia slowly differentiated and built up their own language, their own world, and even their own consciousness and their own psychology. We ourselves have slowly evolved, unfolded and differentiated everything *from the inside*, as it were – and we are still doing so. We are the only world-makers, so that *our* world is in effect the only world. No other being has evolved a complete world around itself, as we have. Animals have only an environment of sensations: we build around ourselves a complete world of values and meanings – a highly-organized, coherent world.

Even more striking, our world has been so completely delivered to us that there is no longer any other class of being that seriously threatens us, or disputes our possession of our world. There are no longer any aliens, evil spirits, ghosts or monsters. They have been reduced to the status of children's bogies, and the old fearsome beasts that used to be shot on sight – gorillas, tigers, polar bears and the like – are now cherished and protected.

Interestingly, it is quite common in the old American creation myths for the world to be created in and by the thinking of a *human* primal father. He struggles awake, his thought becomes more differentiated – and the world gradually takes shape. See, for example, the myths of the Winnebago Earthmaker, and the Uitoto of Colombia.[4] Equally good is the old North-Canadian myth of the Raven, which pictures the primal void as a jet-black raven crouched sleeping in total darkness. Gradually the Raven awakens and a glimmer of light appears: gradually he **makes out** the world – and again we see that the cosmology of a tribal society can be *philosophically* much superior to the religious and scientific cosmologies of the more recent civilizations, including our own. The myths understand what our own clever contemporaries cannot understand – that the creation of the objective world cannot be distinguished from, *and is in effect the same process as*, our own gradual development of language, consciousness and a differentiated world-picture. Does anyone nowadays really think that we can compare our physics with Absolute Physics, our cosmology with the way the world is absolutely? No: we have no basis for making any distinction between *our* world and *the* world. In practice we are of course obliged to equate the world-picture that *we* have developed with the way the world actually *is*, while acknowledging that the cosmos nowadays is not a fixed and God-given fact, but a very light and changeable human construct. This practical equation of *our* world with *the* world is what Hilary Putnam calls 'internal realism', and I call 'human realism'. Hence, by the way, the truth in the Indian idea of *karma*: our entire world-picture, including all our habits of perception, description and interpretation, is a human historical product. We are to blame for it all; such as it is, we made it. It may be a poor thing, so far; but it's our own.

Gradually, gradually, it has become slowly clearer to us that in the changeover from traditional to late-or-post-modern culture everything, really *everything*, has changed over from being massively solid and god-made to being slowly humanly-evolved and still evolving. (Our language by now shows that we have made the change, but it must be understood that as yet most of us won't admit it explicitly. The point is too difficult to grasp, too difficult even for most of our professional philosophers.)

So the transition to a radical humanist world-view – or, from realism to anti-realism – began with the great German Idealist philosophers, and is still going on. It's the changeover from a solid, god-made and objective created order, moral order and selfhood, to a very much *lighter*, continuously-changing, man-made construction or projection of 'reality' as a mighty shadow cast by the motion of language in the human life-world. It is a stupendous and marvellous change, the single most important thing that every modern human person needs to grasp – and the hardest to grasp.

Nothing is alien to us. No rival beings shape our world. The world is at last understood to be wholly and solely *ours*, completely given to us in a way that annihilates old superstitions and fears. As the Apostle puts it, *All things are yours* (I Corinthians 3.21): and again we understand that the combination of radical humanism, antirealism and semiotic materialism in postmodernity is a fulfilment of ancient religious hopes for a globalized, communicative, ultra-light and completely human world. We are **getting there**, we are **coming through**, we will **make it**. The reason why so many people fail to see this is that they have fetishized church-Christianity, failing to remember that it was only an interim formation, preparing the way for something better that is to follow it. Fortunately, ordinary language is once again rather sharper than are we who use it. It already shows something of what has happened, even before we – its users – fully understand it.

So much for the *first* stage of the secularization of our old other-worldly religious consciousness, namely the transition that began with Comte, Feuerbach and Marx to radical humanism, and the anti-realism that it was to bring in its train. The second stage is the gradual development, especially since around 1860, of a highly 'civilian' mass culture of leisure, no longer under law and discipline in quite the old way.

The resulting cultural change is enormous. Until as late as the 1950s, most people's world-view and ethic was still dominated by the work that consumed most of their time. Work-discipline and the work-ethic were dominant in ideology, and prominent in people's moral and religious vocabulary, simply because in order successfully to complete your course and hand over to the next generation you must maintain your total commitment to work. Life was a struggle for survival that required a strict moral discipline. But from around 1960 there appears a new cultural situation in which great numbers of ordinary people, and especially young people, put very much more effort into how they spend their leisure (and how they look while spending it) than they do into their work.[5] Leisure has become more important than employment because people now have much more spending-power, in a situation where full-time employment consumes only about half their waking hours during only about half of their lives. And even people to whom their work remains very important are conscious of a great change. In the old order one worked to live and lived to work. All life was governed by the demands of work, and one looked for 'rest' in the Hereafter; whereas in the new order the epochs of work and rest, history and post-history, are interwoven. Two different worlds, and two surprisingly different world-views. One is aware of oscillating between them every day, every week.

It is hard to remember now, but in the past the church was 'militant' and the lower-ranking member of the church was a *miles Christi*, a soldier of Christ, subject to church law and under authority. Everyone understood that in time of war when one joins the army, one must accept strict discipline and obedience to superiors. But since World War Two our liberal democracies have become *very* civilian and consumerist in their values. People have become most reluctant to give unquestioning obedience to authorities who propose to tell them what to believe and how to live. They want to decide these things for themselves.

In our leisure culture, morality has already changed radically. An old vocabulary – *the moral law, conscience, duty, obedience, loyalty, principle, authority, tradition, elders and betters, merit, right and wrong, 'ought' and obligation* – that entire vocabulary has largely passed out of use,[6] being replaced by a new morality of human rights – a morality of **lifestyle**, **'pride'**, and **free self-expression**. Everyone, male and female alike, demands the **freedom** and the **right** to **come out** – that is, **to do his own thing** and **to live her own life**. The term **lifestyle** is highly antinomian: its popularity signifies a nearly-complete rejection of law-ethics, in favour of the right to conduct one's own life in a manner uniquely one's own that one has freely chosen for oneself. *My life* equals *my symbolic self-expression*, or my 'objectivity': my own *show*. This *show* of ours, that we want to put on in our leisure time, is of vital religious and moral importance to us. **I want to control my own life**, people say, and **make my own decisions**. My life isn't mine unless *I* make the decisions about it. I want to be the teller of my own life-story. And the only limitation I acknowledge is that which is imposed by my recognition that every other person deserves the same expressive freedom that I claim for myself. Each person's life should be their own lived free speech. Everyone wants to make a contribution: everyone wants to gain recognition. Everyone should have the chance to **put on a good show** of their own.

This new morality could not have come into being *as a mass movement* until greater prosperity and shorter working hours had created a society in which the masses have a good deal of leisure time that is very important to them. But since the late 1950s we *have* come to live in a leisure society, and the new ethic is quite clearly *not* a disciplinarian ecclesiastical ethic on the military model, but a kingdom ethic, suited for the millennial time of 'rest' that follows the end of the long war. We are out of uniform now, and in our demob suits: we have a new post-Law world to build.

Do people remember now that in the old Christian cosmology the world was to last for seven aeons, then thought of as periods of 1000 years, each corresponding to one day of the Creator's week? This cosmology was widely and seriously believed till the seventeenth century, and remembered till the nineteenth. There were 4000 years before Christ, Sunday to Wednesday, and 2000 'years of our Lord', the years of grace after Christ. This was the period of the church militant, Thursday and Friday of the cosmic week, the age of mediated religion during which people would be soldiers on the Long March (*in via*), sustained by the iron rations of dogmatic belief and sacramentally-channelled grace. Then in the year 2000 history would end and the true millennium, the 1000-year cosmic sabbath, would begin. It is what the Bible calls the 'rest' of the saints, originally in the promised land after the wilderness wanderings (Deuteronomy 12.9; Psalm 95.11), but now, from the year 2000, 'rest' in an age of leisure and religious fulfilment in the presence of Christ after the hard labour of church history. The expectation was that all the disciplinary apparatus of organized, mediated religion – the compulsory creeds, the hierarchy, the canon law, the sacraments – would decay, as being no longer required. Ordinary human lives would no longer be spent in hard labour, in working clothes, and in the service of various pastors and masters: life would be like one long fancy-dress party, with people choosing to dress themselves in a way that tickles their fancy and expresses their personality.

Until quite recently, people did believe all this, and were

familiar with biblical texts such as Hebrews 4.9f. that teach it. The 'rest' of the ancient Israelites in the promised land was not the final rest, says the author. There is a greater rest yet to come: 'So then, there remains a sabbath rest for the people of God; for whoever enters God's rest also ceases from his labours as God did from his.' And that 'rest' was long and widely expected to begin with the return of Christ in the year of grace 2000.

But it is already 2000, and perhaps we have jumped the gun: for I am again suggesting that there are very notable connections between postmodern philosophy and kingdom theology, connections between radical humanism, anti-realism, and the birth of a postmodern leisure culture that has replaced the traditional law-morality with an expressionist lifestyle-ethics, and which loves the old language of **Eden, paradise** and **heaven on earth**. It is as if the old disciplinary view of life as hard labour is now perceived to be passing away, taking with it all the ideas about religion and morality that it generated. To use the old theological jargon for a moment, our 'eschatology has been realized', as the future world has come forward into the present and the posthistorical time of rest has arrived in our time. The old long-termism – hard labour under strict supervision now, to be followed by rest and reward hereafter – has been replaced by the new short-termist leisure culture of instant happiness and **heaven on earth** that trumpets its promises to us in all the glossy magazines on the news-stands. Notice the striking fact that there are no popular work-magazines. The glossies are all about, and only about, leisure. If you say *I Want it Now*,[7] the magazines reply that *You can indeed have it now*. Nowadays we don't use the word heaven in connection with life after death; we use it in connection with a state of exalted joy and guiltless happiness that is reached here and there in this life.

This new consumerist leisure culture first appeared amongst the middle classes in the 1860s or so, French Impressionist painting being a witness to it. Amongst the masses, it began to appear in the USA in the 1920s, but more confidently and permanently in the 1950s, and then first fully grasped its own revolutionary character at the height of the late 1960s. For one reason and another, the Australians latched on to it rather earlier than most, but its full implications are still unfolding. During the 1990s there was a fresh surge, in which again we see postmodern philosophy developing hand-in-hand with post-ecclesiastical religion. Our postmodernity represents the final stage in the historical development of Christianity.

Derrida has described deconstruction as an activity. It is not as if he personally invented deconstructive analysis as a *technique*, which then spread through the culture like a new technology, as he and his followers applied it to one topic after another. Rather, we should see him as describing a process, a spontaneous activity that has been going on in the culture during his time and ours, as all the old disciplinary structures, hierarchies, oppositions, distinctions, value-scales, beings and laws have been disintegrating, coming apart, scattering and splashing. It's been happening in philosophy, in ethics, in politics, in religion and in art. Its effect is nihilistic, in that the old objective realities and contrasts – moral, religious, metaphysical – disintegrate, melt away and are scattering; and it is also sacralizing, because value and holiness are no longer so concentrated or tightly clumped as they used to be, nor are they located in an imaginary world above. They are scattered across the whole human lifeworld, and may be met with almost anywhere.

The result attracts sharply-conflicting assessments. If you have been a member of the armed forces you will recall and understand the professional soldier's contempt for the civilian world: it seems to him slack, shapeless, self-indulgent and half-asleep. In Civvy Street, nobody is alert and nothing has a clear outline. Anything goes: and in just the same way intellectual, religious and moral conservatives who were raised in the old disciplinarian culture see postmodernity as being a morass of relativism, a world that has no standards and has lost its way. The postmodern religious person who rejects ecclesiastical discipline – i.e., 'orthodoxy' – is seen as one who 'believes nothing'. The postmodern philosopher who rejects Enlightenment rationalism is seen as one who has rejected reason outright, and as being unable to distinguish between 'argument' and 'rhetoric'.[8]

The postmodern moralist who rejects talk of absolute values and prefers to say that we do and must continually criticize and reinvent our values is seen as denying values altogether.

So the surviving disciplinarians reject the new world that has been coming into being since the 1960s; whereas those who like and feel at home in the new era see the conservatives as unhappy lovers, hopelessly attached to a cruel and repressive cultural order from which we are delighted to have been delivered. What they see as religious decline, we see as religious fulfilment.

2

Different Perceptions

As we change over from a culture dominated by the need to maintain work discipline, toiling now in the expectation of rest and reward 'hereafter', to a culture dominated by lifestyle and an expressivist ethic of self-realization by public display – **coming out, doing one's own thing, strutting one's stuff**, and trying to **put on a good show**[1] – so people's sense of reality changes, and the world itself changes.

The old metaphysical realism was closely associated with the idea that when we **come into this world** we come into an antecedently-fixed and effectively-immutable disciplinary moral framework. Our chief task is not to attract attention to ourselves, but merely to **fit in** and quietly do our duty. Thomas Cranmer's English Catechism of 1549 (which was, in only slightly revised form, authoritative until very recently) conveys very well a certain traditional conception of the good life:

> *Question.* What is thy dutie towardes thy neighboure?
> *Answere.* My duetie towardes my neighbour is, to loue hym as myselfe. And to do to al men as I would they should do to me. To loue, honour, and succoure my father and mother. To honour and obey the kyng and his ministers. To submitte myselfe to all my gouernours, teachers, spirituall pastours, and maisters. To ordre myselfe lowlye and reuerentelye to al my betters. To hurte no bodie by woorde nor dede. To bee true and iust in al my dealing. To beare no malice nor hatred in my heart. To kepe my handes from picking and stealing, and my tongue from euill speaking, liyng, and slaundring. To kepe my bodie in temperaunce, sobreness, and

chastitie. Not to couet nor desire other mennes goodes. But learne and laboure truly to geate my owne liuing, and to doe my duetie in that state of life: unto which it shal please God to cal me.[2]

Inevitably, moral realism at the cosmic level is here closely associated with respect for the social order. Politically, realism is close to Toryism. Equally inevitably, the disciplinary vision of the world is patriarchal. Woman's concern for appearances and self-presentation (*How do I look?*) was regarded as 'vanity', and the more religious a woman was, the more her dress had to approximate to a very sober uniform. Holding forth over lunch, a rather elderly academic friend of mine (whom I will of course not name) declared sententiously that 'Woman is primitive man'. 'Less lateralized', he added. He meant things like divergent thinking, and indeed mythical thinking. I was clearly expected to cap this remark, so I replied: 'Woman is postmodern man', referring to her love of appearances and of the passing show of existence. From one point of view woman is more archaic than man, and from the other point of view woman is more highly-developed than man.

Against this background, the transition to the newer expressionist or **lifestyle** ethics can be seen to involve a very marked feminization of the whole culture. Today, your self is your **image**. Your 'personality' is no longer something inward and spiritual that is concealed behind a sober exterior, but rather is seen as realizing itself in your self-presentation, your dress and your **lifestyle-choices** in a whole range of areas – fashion, travel, books, food, design, home and garden, music and the arts, and so forth. Instead of *wanting to be good* in the old way, **one aspires to a lifestyle**. Metaphysically, the old objective Order-out-there is replaced by a flux of ambiguous, teasing appearances, as everything pours out and passes away. Postmodernity combines symbolic abundance with metaphysical minimalism.

By enacting your lifestyle (journalists nowadays often use the regrettable phrase **living a lifestyle**) you generate a world around yourself. It is your familiar surroundings, your territory, marked with your personal style just as an animal's territory is marked with its scent. It is your own distinctive 'take' or 'angle' on and your personal contribution to the human lifeworld as a whole. In my jargon, your little world that you establish around yourself is your expressed 'objectivity', and even your work of art. It is legible, being made of signs, because all human expression is symbolic. In everything you do you are **sending out messages,** and **making a statement** about yourself. So the human lifeworld as a whole is a flux of signs, to which each of us is making a contribution; and it is the primary world, within which and on the basis of which the various more specialized worlds are constructed.

In a film of 1955, *The Night My Number Came Up*, scripted by R. C. Sherriff, occurs a very early use of the phrase **We have a duty to life, to live it to the full.** 'A duty to life': the phrase strikingly conveys the unstoppable determination of postmodern young people to choose their own style, their own fashions and their own manner of self-presentation. With great religious tenacity, they insist that they will **have it their own way.** And that really *is* religion, now. It is no longer a matter of self-denial and submission to order and discipline: it's a matter of feeling impelled to **come out** and **do one's own thing, in one's own way.** Because they don't understand the change that has occurred, older people talk disapprovingly about the *me-generation* and *making an exhibition of yourself*. They fail to grasp that whereas ecclesiastical religion was disciplinary, kingdom religion is expressivist. It is often supposed that ordinary people are naive realists about the public world, and that they would find incomprehensible the notion that we are the makers of the world. But ordinary people very often voice the moral ambition to **leave the world a little bit better place than I found it,** which implies that they fully understand how we ourselves continually make and remake it. The world is each generation's legacy to the next. In the same spirit people may say to their children: **'I'm afraid our generation have left a bit of a mess, and it will be up to your generation to do better than we did.'** Certainly in the twentieth century, after the physical and moral devastation caused by the two World Wars, the idea of setting out to rebuild a ruined world became familiar to millions.

Ordinary language, I suggest, is *not* naïvely realist about 'the world' and our perceptions of it. In ordinary language the world is in effect the human world, which is the human lifeworld, which is the product of all our symbolic self-expression. Mobile telephones are currently being advertised with the slogan: **It was never so easy to take your world with you.** Your world comprises your circle of friends and everything you chatter about with them; and you need to be in constant touch. To quote another advertising slogan, your mobile telephone gives you **The world in your pocket.** The world changes so fast nowadays that styles are felt to change profoundly, not just in each generation, but in each decade, and even each *year*. It is hard work to keep up. This implies that if we want to know what's going on in the world around us we must do more than passively *register* our sense-experience: we must say our piece; we must **join the show**, and interpret it *perceptively*. The world is not made of bare objective facts known through the senses, because a mere sensory stimulus by itself has no meaning and can tell us nothing. In practice, the world has to be *read*, and is made of *signs and interpretations*: and during the past few decades the word **perception** has indeed come to be used of a particular way of understanding or interpreting something. For example, if we seek to bring about social change in some area, we will often say that we need to challenge 'common perceptions' of such and such. 'That may be **the way you see it**, but it's not **the way I see it.**' Or again, if we are interested in relations between the US and China, we may attempt to describe each country's **perception** of the other. It is important to try to understand the other person's perception of the situation because, more than some people like to admit, the whole political world is actually made up of conflicting perceptions, and we cannot hope to settle the argument by appealing to an objective truth beyond all the perceptions. There isn't one: there is only the conflict of perceptions. You cannot sensibly ask which country's view of the world is the true one. Diplomats have to be relativists. **That's life.** We don't have

it in itself: we have only **the way it looks to you** and **the way it looks to me**. We don't have the world absolutely; only various **world-views**. And we don't have objective realities out there; only appearances.

In this way, then, our experience of major ideological conflict, and of the difficulty of changing entrenched attitudes, has in recent years been tilting ordinary language towards anti-realism. If you want to join a social group, or to make progress in international relations, or simply to make friends with someone of the opposite sex, you must get into the habit of interpreting signals of many kinds, you must be aware of the way your own subjectivity contributes to your own interpretations, and you must give up the ideas of a ready-made objective truth about human relations and a ready-made criterion of rights and wrongs. The world consists of different interpretations and viewpoints. Whether we are talking about a man and a woman, or about the United States and China, there's his perception and there's her perception, and there is *no* perspectiveless or absolute vision accessible to us. There is no Last Judgment or Final Truth: there is only the play of different interpretations – and our occasional great happiness when, now and again, and **in spite of it all**, we find ourselves unexpectedly and completely **at one**.

Supra-history, an idea that crops up here and there in recent philosophy, is the idea that after we've given up the belief in historical progress towards a final attainment of absolute truth, we can find the point of life in those almost-transcendent moments now and again when **it all makes sense**, and **we are at one**. Now and again, everything briefly comes together: perhaps when the subjective and objective realms are in full harmony, or when I and thou are at one, suddenly, **it all makes sense** – and **it's heaven**.

If, however, ordinary language has become very aware of *perspectivism* and the anti-realism to which it leads, what are we to make of the continuing bias towards realism in much Anglo-Saxon philosophy and natural science? They define *perception* as the ability to see, hear, or become aware of things through the senses. More exactly, it is the word that is used of the neurophysiological processes, including reference to memory, by which an organism converts sensory stimuli into information about the external world. The definitions *presuppose* a common public world of material bodies, and picture the sense-organs as receptors through which a body that has them gains information about other bodies. Notice that science *always presupposes, and therefore can never prove*, that there is such a world, and that the senses give us information about it. Descartes compared the impression that an external body may make upon one of my senses with the impression that a seal may make upon soft wax – thus conveying the idea that perception is most accurate when it is most 'soft' and passive, so that the sense-organ receives a clear imprint like a little picture of the thing perceived. And the puzzle is that a good deal of scientific practice still seems to be reliant upon a commonsense-realist account of perception along such lines as these, especially in its ideas about trained observers and their observations, even while research in psychology is moving further and further away from any sort of realist account of perception. The human sciences, and especially cognitive science, are developing a very uncomfortable internal contradiction. Psychological research is done upon realist assumptions that are undermined by its conclusions.

The extreme case is human visual processing, accounts of which have become prodigiously complex in recent years.[3] Read an account of the current state of theory, and reflect that the people who have produced these theories, and *you yourself also as you peruse these lines*, are caught up in all these complications. Everyone is. None of us ever has access to the external world except via this elaborate machinery. So nobody is in a position to check all this: nobody is or can be in a position to check what visible things actually look like, objectively and apart from what is done to them as they are processed by the human visual system. Each of us is always inside his own visual system, and cannot step out of it to check its accuracy. So the psychologists must be proceeding by the transcendental method: given that we are physical bodies moving about in a physical world, and given that our visual system does evidently guide us around pretty successfully, we analyse backwards and argue that *this* must be how it is working. Thus current psychology makes an initial presumption of metaphysical realism, and then develops very complex theories about how we must be processing our visual experience, if our visual system is (most of the time) to serve us as well as it evidently does. As for the *truth* of these theories of visual processing – well, they'll be justified pragmatically. Correspondence is clearly out of the question. Furthermore, the initial presumption of realism can of course never be justified. All one is ever going to be able to say is that a general philosophical presumption of realism is commonsense, and works out satisfactorily in practice because, for example, we can most of the time distinguish clearly enough between veridical perceptions and optical illusions to be able to get by.

What modern psychology shows very clearly is that *both* the initial presumption of metaphysical realism *and* the body of special psychological theories that seek to explain perception and other forms of cognition can never be justified more than pragmatically. But pragmatic truth – 'it works out OK in practice, for the moment' – is metaphysically neutral. It is equally compatible with realism, idealism, phenomenalism and our own postmodern anti-realism.

From this I conclude that the present philosophical situation of scientific theories is unstable and unsatisfactory. Many people in the scientific community are vociferously attached to a form of realism or 'objectivism' that they must always assume and therefore can never justify. Rather as we found earlier that in matters of theology ordinary language is sharper and more up-to-date than the professional theologians, so also in matters of metaphysics and the philosophy of science ordinary language is very often sharper and more up-to-date than the professional scientists – and the word **perception** is a case in point.

3

Get Real!

Get real! people exclaim: **You're not living in the real world.** We need now to spell out exactly how 'reality' has changed during the past two centuries or so – what it was, and what it has now become.

Usually, realism in philosophy is taken to be the doctrine that some thing (or class of things) exists, or that some proposition (or class of propositions) is true, in an objective or absolute way – that is, it is 'real', it is true, it exists, quite apart from and independently of its relation to the mind, or to experience, or to language. Its truth is independent of the means by which we might set out to determine its truth. It just is *so*, out-there, by itself and apart from us.

Very well – but if so, then what *is* real in this sense? One might think that matter is a possible candidate. Isn't thoroughgoing materialism a form of realism?

One complication needs to be set aside at once. In ordinary language a materialist is often an acquisitive or miserly person who values money above all else. But money as 'a current medium of exchange' is obviously not real in the sense stipulated. Gold, just lying about in the earth, is not money until somebody finds it, picks it up and takes it into a social context in which it can function as money. Money – like God, as Moses Hess remarked long ago – depends upon people's *belief* in it; that is, their acceptance and observance of all the social rules that establish what it is and how it can be used. Money is not material, but conventional: it's made of signs and rules. Money is highly 'non-realist', just like God (as I have been trying to explain, without much success, for over twenty years).

That complication having been duly set aside, what does a materialist consider to be 'real' and 'self-existent'? Philosophers have always been highly aware of how very fast-changing sense-experience is, and how physical bodies may change state under the action of water, or extreme cold or heat. Matter seems to be fluid, mutable stuff. So what is it that endures? The earliest Greek philosophers soon tried out the main options: the eternity of the world as a whole, the eternity of matter as kind of stuff, the eternity of atoms-and-the-void. But because matter-as-such is so evidently changeable and unstable, the main tradition decided to follow Plato's solution, which was to ascribe reality not to matter itself but to the various intelligible Forms that may be impressed upon it to make it into a fairly-stable physical thing of one kind or another. This solution was eventually to lead away not just from materialism but from any sort of realism, for it subordinates the world of sense-experience to the intellectual world of 'Ideas': thought-forms, patterns, concepts, meanings – all of which have in recent years come to be seen as human contrivances. And in any case, straight materialism has not been a very popular position in the history of philosophy, Eastern or Western. There are too many objections to it. Nowadays, physics is not quite materialist and does not quite teach the conservation of matter. On the contrary, all particles have a finite life-span. Amongst philosophers – especially on the European Continent, where the Marxist vocabulary has been most influential – the term materialism is no longer strictly connected with matter *at all*, and has instead come to be used as a synonym for what Anglo-Saxons usually prefer to call naturalism.

So much for the term materialism. More significant has been the huge influence upon the philosophical tradition of the idea of God the Creator. What kind of reality is ascribed to God, and what sort and degree of reality did being-created-by-God gain for the world?

Certainly the main tradition was realist about God. God's reality showed itself in his supreme and dreadful power and authority, manifest in the whole created order and notably in such created witnesses to it as absolute monarchy and the faculty of conscience.

Mystics, and the negative theologians, in various ways qualified classical theistic realism. They were sharply opposed to anthropomorphism, to the point at which they would insist that we have no positive knowledge at all about God – *except* that he exists. We don't know *what* God is, they often said, but we do know *that* God is. You may not care for that form of words (and I certainly do not), but it does show that they *were* still realists – at least, in intention, and at least, usually.

All of which reveals that in the great theistic traditions God's reality meant in the end one thing only: even if we could know nothing about it, there was, because there *had* to be, a single ultimate source of all power and authority that founded, made real and validated everything.

René Descartes makes the same point very clearly. In his view the (human) natural philosopher can in principle give a complete account of the physical world. We can know it all as completely as God knows it all. So what is the difference between a complete mathematical description of nature and the actual existence of nature? Simple, answers Descartes: the power of God[1] – and here the general truth emerges. In the theistic traditions, 'reality', the actual existence of things, is simply an effect of power, the infinite power that God has and we lack. As theologians are wont to say, the world *minus* the power of God equals zero. God's power is the sole producer and sustainer of actual reality. We all know it: nothing can be more terribly *real* to me than that which has unlimited power over me.

It follows that in the main traditions of Christendom and Islam your sense of the objective reality of the world about you was always a function of your sense of the power of God, holding everything together in being. What God said, went: reality was, as it always is, a function of legislative power and authority. The supreme Lawgiver was the Supreme Being. But then, as during the eighteenth century God began to seem an unnecessary hypothesis and to fade away, so the fixed objective reality of the world began to fade too, opening a space for the Romantic Movement and the philosophy of Kant.

At that moment the nature of reality began to change. People had seen themselves as the spectators of a fully-determinate law-governed Cosmos, held in objective existence by the continuous exertion of God's infinite power. Now they began to see the world as taking shape in their own knowing of it, as their minds processed the raw and formless data of experience and an ordered world appeared. They began to see that it is through our human conversation that we differentiate experience and generate the human life-world around ourselves. They began to see that *we* give all the orders, and that poets are *the unacknowledged legislators of the world.*[2] They began to see the creative artist as the pioneer of culture, and as a role-model for us all as a world-builder. And instead of seeing the world as a cosmos that was made and finished in the beginning, they began to think of *the world as history*, as the historically-evolving human life-world. The slow evolution of our communal thinking, our culture, is always also the evolution of our world-view, and so in effect of the world itself.

What then happens to reality? In the old order, as we saw, the cosmos was as real and objective as your sense of the almighty power of God, upholding it in reality. In the new order, the world is basically the human life-world, and it is as real as your sense of the power and authority of our public conversational consensus. If you are language-minded, you will, like Wittgenstein, be impressed by what a very large amount of common ground our language gives us, and how very strong a thing the current consensus is. But we have also had to accustom ourselves to the realization that it is a *shifting* consensus. Cosmology and morality were both of them markedly different when I was a boy. They really were.

When ordinary language tells someone to **get real** and to **join the real world**, it is instructing him to look to the public consensus. It is warning him not to walk about **with his head in the clouds**. Don't be content to **live in a world of your own**: you need to interlock your world with the worlds of others. Don't be dreamy and solipsistic; look to the language and world-view of ordinariness. It is all we've got, it is our world, it is **reality**. Hence, **take a reality-check!**

So: reality now is carried within and sustained by our human conversational consensus. Language goes all the way down; language forms our experience from the very beginning; our language builds the human world as *the* world. By way of supporting evidence I cite the changing use of the term 'world'. Between the sixteenth and early nineteenth centuries it was quite commonly used of the planet earth, or of the solar system, as well as of the cosmos. One talked about, for example, 'the Copernican system of the world'. But nowadays we describe the cosmos of the astronomers simply as *the universe*, and the term *world* is used almost exclusively with reference to the human world – the world of **world history**, the world of human society, the human life-world and its many and varied sub-worlds, such as the worlds of dog-breeders, and of policemen. The set of moral assumptions prevailing in a world has recently come to be called its *culture*. Thus people speak of **police culture**, and they are not referring to the musical taste of policemen.

'Reality', now, is the way things are, the way things go, and the assumptions that are carried, within the human social world. As evidence, here are the thirty-five or so currently most prominent world-idioms:

All the world's a stage (Shakespeare)
a world away from (= in a very different sub-world: cp. **worlds apart**)
the hand that rocks the cradle rules the world
the world, the flesh and the Devil
one half of the world doesn't know how the other half lives
laugh, and the world laughs with you
coming down in the world / going up in the world
he's not of this world / he lives in a world of his own
he's not long for this world
she has the world at her feet
the best of both worlds

a man of the world
world-weary / world-shattering / world-famous
the world as we know it
he carries the world before him
bring into the world (give birth, or assist in the birth of)
Love makes the world go round
the world is your oyster (= you will easily gain social advancement)
the world is my parish (John Wesley, *Journal*)
a world of difference (= a difference as great as the difference beween one social sub-world and another)
tout le monde (= everyone, **The world and his wife**)
the world over (= amongst people everywhere)
the world owes me a living
it takes all sorts to make a world
this world (= this life, as in **Not long for this world**)
the world well lost (= social position sacrificed without regret)
the world would be a poorer place (. . . without her, or people like her)
world without end / the end of the world (= the end of history)
world history, world spirit (after Hegel)
worldly wise (compare *streetwise*)
the best of all possible worlds (Leibniz's *Theodicy*; Voltaire's *Candide*)
God's in his heaven / All's right with the world (Browning)

In this list[3] the *only* world-idioms that are, or might be understood as being, cosmological are found amongst the ones that are quotations from writers of the past. Otherwise, *all* of our current world-idioms refer to the human social world. The only notable (and partial) exception is the expressive use of *the world* to signify total astonishment, or unlimited feeling generally:

where in the world did you get that hat?
she thinks the world of him
the world well lost
out of this world (= superlatively good)

for all the world as if . . .
it means the world to me (= everything)
why in the world did he do that?

We should compare what has happened to **the world** with what has happened to **God**. The world in the sense of the cosmos has faded along with God; but *the human social world has come forward to replace the old cosmos*. In ordinary language, then, the world is now the human world, and the human consensus is now our criterion of reality. **The natural world** is a sub-world within the human world, and those who study it work by striving to obtain a consensus-view of it. The old subjective-objective distinction has changed into the newer private-public distinction: for us, now, public-ation equals real-ization.

The gradual shift from a God-made objective real world to the newer view of reality as held within a human conversational consensus is paralleled by a similar shift in the character of our knowledge – a shift which many people will regard as a dreadful comedown. From the fourth to the eleventh centuries the dominant sort of knowledge was *sapientia*, divine wisdom. From the thirteenth to the sixteenth, it was dogmatic theology, sacred knowledge. From the seventeenth to the nineteenth centuries it was natural philosophy, human scientific knowledge. And now at the end of the twentieth century it is simply 'information', data that is stored in machines. One may say facetiously that knowledge **has come down in the world**, just as *the world itself has come down in the world*. And coming down *in the world* is coming down *socially*.

This change has somewhat ironized the older cosmic-religious uses of the word *world*, in phrases such as **the Creator of the world** and **the Saviour of the world**. The irony shows up in the way a modern environmental activist is somewhat sardonically spoken of by others as '**busy saving the world**'.

Oddly, church leaders are often rather unaware of linguistic change, and I think I have never heard or read a modern discussion of whether 'the world' that Christ has saved is the whole cosmos, or simply the human social world.

4

The Religious Character of Postmodern Experience

People who are psychologically troubled often feel that they have been taken over by some alien power. They may undergo very abrupt changes of state, alternating between the highest exaltation and the deepest despair. The extremes that they experience are so great that only religious language is sufficiently dramatic to express what they have felt. In them, language has run riot.

So it is in postmodernity: living as we do after history, after the breakdown of the authority of the great disciplinary institutions[1] and their orthodoxies, after the Law therefore, and after deference, we have become very highly reflexively-conscious and unillusioned. We have **seen through** everything: '**Been there, done that.**' We are to a great degree emancipated from the old disciplines, rituals and routines that formerly burdened us, controlled us and, as they say, **kept us on the rails**. We have been demobilized, and are as a result *both* much freer *and* much less stable. In our generation extremes of experience that in the past were accessible only to a very few highly exceptional creative people have suddenly become thoroughly democratized.[2] Many people who in other days might have been very glad to settle for a quiet life unexpectedly find themselves falling apart, roller-coasting from the highest heaven to the pit of hell. So they have said to me, and I know exactly what they mean.

It is not surprising, therefore, that religious phrases and images are as ubiquitous in ordinary language today, and above all perhaps in popular art, as they are in the poetry of

Christopher Smart and William Blake. We are so emancipated and so nihilistic that, like the painter Francis Bacon, we are theological again. If you thought that by getting rid of 'organized religion' we would somehow solve the problem of religion, you've got another think coming. As Thomas Hobbes and others well understood, the historical function of 'organized religion' was not somehow to invent religion and foist it upon the people, but rather to discipline and tame the violence of religion, and try to direct it along socially-useful channels. What people call 'the decline of religion' is very often merely the decay of the guiding institutions that used to control religious language and provided innocent outlets for religious energies. Inevitably, the result is a violent upsurge of almost-psychotic religion – fundamentalist, charismatic, pentecostal, sectarian and ethno-nationalist.[3] As may be seen from California to Kensington, even relatively highly-educated people may succumb to the influence of such movements.

In addition to the upsurge of aggressively disorderly religion as a political force, there is also a big return in postmodernity of technically-religious language and symbolism. We are not talking here about blasphemies and profanities, which are common in all ages, and we are not talking merely of the way in which ordinary conversation may still be peppered with biblical phrases like **pass by on the other side, den of thieves, pearly gates**, and **straight and narrow**. Nor, again, are we here talking about the many pious-sounding sayings that are still frequently heard, such as **Make a clean breast of it, Bridle your tongue, Charity begins at home** and **Be thankful for small mercies**. We should also discount the religious words that have come into ordinary language from anthropology, such as **tribe, totem, myth, magic, witch doctor, trance** and **taboo**. What we are looking for is rather the unexpected return of specifically-religious or theological signs that have come back because only they are sufficiently powerful to articulate the extremity of postmodern spiritual life.

For example, not many years ago people learning to pray were taught that one's daily devotions should move through four main stages, summed up by the acronym ACTS: adoration, confession, thanksgiving and supplication. All four of these religious attitudes are now dispersed and widespread in secular life, despite the traditional theological ban on directing towards creatures feelings and attitudes whose proper object is God alone.

1. **Adoration**
   they're devoted to each other
   she idolizes him
   he worships her (in a stronger sense than is implied in the English marriage-vows, where to worship is simply to honour)
   I adore her
   A **venerated** elder statesman

I think that nobody raises any objection to this transfer of the language of religious worship into personal relationships – even when it becomes hyperbolic, as in **He worships the ground beneath her feet** (or **the ground she walks on**). Old people are ready to smile indulgently over **the cult of the worship of Abba** (a phrase I noticed yesterday), over **celebrity-worship**, and even over the treatment of **rock memorabilia as sacred relics**. But a noticeable edge of disapproval attends the use of phrases such as **the religion of shopping**, the description of shopping malls as **temples of shopping**, and **the Sunday morning ritual of washing the family car**. It seems that we are entirely happy to see religious language spreading through the personal realm, but have kept something of the old Protestant dislike of idolatry when we see people getting seriously religious about money, shopping, consumption and cars. In which case what seems to have happened is that the old infinite qualitative distinction between God and all that is not God has been quietly transformed into a new religious distinction between the human world and the non-human realm of **it**.[4] You can get as religious as you wish about anything human, and – within limits – you will also be indulged in the case of objects that are or have been very closely associated with humans, such as memorabilia of the stars, and pet animals. (The treatment as **sacred** of the turf at football grounds is perhaps **pushing it a bit.**)

2. **Confession**
   I feel guilty
   I beg your pardon
   I need to get it off my chest
   a sin against the light
   forgive me!
   absolution, atonement, reparation, restitution, satisfaction

John Henry Newman, in typically nineteenth-century style, argued that the vocabulary of shame and guilt, of sin, repentance, confession and forgiveness is *both* profoundly true to moral experience *and* clearly implies that there is Someone Above before Whom we feel all these emotions.[5] Today, it seems that the first part of Newman's argument stands, but the second part has collapsed, for in our post-theistic culture almost the whole Christian vocabulary of sin, guilt, confession, pardon and forgiveness survives intact. The big difference is that if we do feel guilty about having hurt someone, we now seek forgiveness not from God but directly from the injured fellow-human. Some penologists currently use the phrase 'restorative justice' to describe the practice of arranging for criminals to meet their victims. It is a striking sign of how humanist we have suddenly become that the idea is so novel. In the Christian era we confessed our sins, not to the persons we had injured by them, but to God, who could not be hurt in any way. And *we never thought this odd*! To cope with other cases we have had to invent a new kind of sin, in which we have **let ourselves down** and have sinned against **our own self-respect**. This kind of sin is sometimes called a **sin against the light**, and we do talk about the difficult task of learning **to forgive oneself.** If like me you still see value in the old God-language you can treat God as a guiding spiritual ideal, an Inner Light, and still speak poetically of seeking forgiveness from the God within.

3. **Thanksgiving**
   I'm **thankful** for that
   I'm glad/grateful to be alive
   Thank God!
   there but for the Grace of God go I

This requires little comment, because I think everyone understands what I have elsewhere called a 'non-objective cosmic gratitude' in which one is simply grateful for life, grateful for sunshine and grateful for this morning. A good phrase for the sense of pure gratitude is **It's an absolute gift!** – the word 'absolute' making the point that the purest gift of all is the gift with no giver.

4. **Supplication**
   I beg you
   I hope to God that . . .
   I hope and pray that you're right
   request, beseech, implore, petition

It might have been expected that acts of petition would disappear in a democratic age, because the supplicant's posture (kneeling, with hands pressed flat together) implies powerlessness addressing one who has absolute power. But prayer as a desperate wish (**I hope to God**) and petitions addressed to those in power remain as much **a part of life** as ever.

– and that is enough; enough to remind us of how the whole range of religious attitudes and feelings, most of which were once directed towards God alone, now flourish dispersed into secular life and giving a religious flavour to much of our experience.

Rather similarly, the comfort and support once given by religious faith may be sought and offered in secular ways. The language of our financial institutions (popularly, **temples of Mammon**) borrows especially from Calvinist theology:

Provident
assurance
mutual
interest (compare 'an interest in my Saviour's blood')
saving
friendly
trust
security
peace of mind[6]

As for the technically religious words and images that return in postmodernity, I have already alluded to the return, in a whole range of painters – some of them avowed atheists – of the Christ-image and the crucifixion, often associated with the triptych, or altarpiece. Some of the best-known examples of this are Gauguin, Ensor, Otto Dix, Max Beckmann, Stanley Spencer, Mark Rothko (for his black triptychs at Houston), Barnett Newman (in his titles), and Francis Bacon. In addition, there are the many artists who have been found to have a taste for Catholic kitsch, and who have a perhaps-teasing way of describing their own art in highly Christian language. They may take pleasure in leaving us in doubt about their seriousness, because in postmodernity our world-view is so fractured that we no longer know for sure what is serious and what isn't. Perhaps everything is superficial and nothing is deep. If so, the artist may enjoy teasing us by experimenting, poker-faced, with religious language and images. Artists who do this have included Warhol, Pierre et Gilles, and Gilbert and George, as well as the egregious (a word meant seriously) Jeff Koons.

We have also discussed already the realization or immanentization in postmodernity of the Last Things, especially **the end of the world, heaven** and **hell**. In addition, **bliss, limbo** and **purgatory** are not forgotten.

Finally, other technical religious terms that have returned in postmodernity (often to be used in new ways) include:

cult
spirit, spirituality

icon
image
charisma
creation
divine, heavenly, godlike
god, goddess (as applied to human beings: 'Shane Warne is my god' – an Australian cricket enthusiast, 1999)
revelation
Bible (as any authoritative book)
miracle
apocalypse
millennium (originally, the 1000-year reign on earth of Christ and his saints)
incarnation
resurrection
the Alpha and Omega
ritual
soul
burnt-offering/holocaust
sacrifice
commandment

These words remind one of the extraordinary tenacity of religious language. In medical matters we are quite happy to change our vocabulary in successive epochs, so that in the sixteenth century *accidie* became *melancholy*, which later became *low spirits*, 'the Black Dog', and then *neurasthenia* and finally *depression*, our own 'malignant sadness'. But in religion the old vocabulary is not forgotten, and keeps coming back, so that, for example, the *initial singularity* in physical cosmology is promptly seized upon by the public as **the moment of Creation.** In religion, more than anywhere else, we cling to the view that the old vocabulary is best, and jump at any opportunity to revive it. And in postmodernity the generation that is more nihilistic than any previous one greatly relishes pious jargon. In a sort of way – nostalgically, non-realistically, ironically – we remain highly religious.

Why? It seems that almost any number of reasons can be given. The late Brian Moore (like very many other novelists, I suspect) wrote Catholic novels all his life without being himself a Catholic believer because he thought that the theological machinery of Catholicism, its mental furniture and its guilty excitements, were **an absolute gift** for the novelist.[7] Rather similarly, Isaac Bashevis Singer was personally always an 'Enlightened' Jew, who (in adult life at least) never shared the outlook of the strangely superstitious and introverted Polish *Hasidim* whom he wrote about. Other artists, like the late film-maker Derek Jarman, greatly relish Catholic art – especially in the Baroque style – for its very high gay and SM content. Perhaps he was 'a spoiled priest', as the phrase used to go.

There is something of that in Francis Bacon too, no doubt; but like others of his generation he may have felt that his own atheism and pessimism was also a religious state – a perpetual Holy Saturday, with God dead, Christ away harrowing hell, and the earth derelict.

The lesson to be learned from artists such as these is that in postmodernity we are all of us – not just liberal believers, but all of us – in an ironized, both-believing-and-unbelieving relation to our own religious tradition. Artists explore and play with the many different nuances of irony now found amongst us, and the fact that they find a public – often, a very large public – shows that we are all of us in varying ways ironized non-realists nowadays. We at-least-half know that it's only myth, but many of us remain very attached to it all nonetheless.

The underlying point here needs to be made more explicit. I say that there is not a single person in the Western (and Western-influenced) world today who is or can be a fully sincere, traditional and orthodox religious believer. The reason for this is that orthodox faith draws its substance or content, so that we know how to *take* it, from the normality *vis-à-vis* which it positions itself, upon which it builds, and which it criticizes, corrects and perfects. But in postmodernity 'normality' is problematic – and therefore so, unavoidably, is faith.

See the point in relation to Catholic Christianity. 'Grace'

builds upon and perfects 'nature'. As long then as we are sure that we know what nature is, our language about grace is anchored to something, and that anchorage helps to give it meaning and 'mindhold'.[8] But in postmodernity, after 'the disappearance of the Real', nature dies. Whatever was it? – It was only a highly mutable cultural fiction, that changed drastically every hundred years or so. But now the end of nature leaves grace up in the air, aestheticized, mythicized, ambivalent. Our theological language no longer *stands on* anything that keeps it in one place.

For the proof of this from ordinary language, notice that when we are travelling our guides *and we ourselves* now commonly use exactly the same light, good-humoured and bracketed or mock-realistic language to describe other people's gods and theologies as we use to describe our own. All belief, our own as well as other people's, is treated with the same odd mixture of overt respect and veiled irony.

So postmodernity is very hospitable. It smiles at all the old ideas of exclusive truth, objective reality and so on, but welcomes everyone under its roof. And when the old religious certainties have been ironized, deconstructed and disseminated – then there is more religion *about* than ever. Floating.

How much does it matter that our old religious vocabulary has become so free-floating? Certainly, it is no longer connected with an established vision of a ready-made law-governed cosmos, and therefore it no longer has the power to *constrain* us morally in quite the old way. But I have in any case been arguing *against* moral realism. There is no moral order out there that tells us the rules by which we must live. All of us know in our hearts nowadays that 'the universe' is objectively meaningless, and morality is only human. In the old world the cosmic moral order, *via* religious symbolism, bound us to a certain law-governed pattern of life. Not any more, though: in postmodernity deconstructed and free-floating religious symbols have become freely available to us all for incorporation *ad lib* into our lifestyles. Solar ethics is not a form of law-ethics, grounded in a vision of a cosmic moral order: it is purely expressive and theatrical. So we can just *choose* to live in and through religious symbols, as a girl may just *choose* to wear a little gold cross on a chain about her neck. Why not?

At this point many people become irritable, because they baulk at the magnitude of the change that we are going through. The old world-view was realistic in cosmology, theology and morality. Religion was a matter of slotting yourself into a vast ready-made cosmic order that surrounded you and had a place prepared for you. When all that goes, religion ceases to be a way of responding to reality and becomes instead a mere matter of lifestyle, a way of generating reality. My religious vocabulary used to choose *me*, and required me to live in the way that it commanded; now I choose *it*, as the vocabulary in which I want to express myself. But when I say this I seem to the traditionalists to be turning everything inside out, to be putting the cart before the horse in every possible way. What I am saying seems to them to be unintelligible. (They know I'm right, but they really *hate* it, and will not admit it.)

5

Postmodern Religious Belief

I have been suggesting that, in the Roman Catholic vocabulary, 'grace needs nature': that is, any traditional type of religious system borrows its meaning, its 'mindhold', and its effectiveness in practice, from the normality that it presupposes, symbolizes, criticizes and seeks imaginatively to transform. But in postmodernity Nature, the *base*, has become problematic. The things we formerly supposed to be 'real' have turned out to be made of signs all the way down, and we never get hold of a pure base, independent of the signs. All we feel philosophically sure of is the flux of signs, spreading like ripples over the surface of our attention, and out of which we construct our many and varied pictures of the world out there and the self in here. And if we are nowadays very doubtful about the solidity and permanence of any notion of 'the Real' beyond or outside language, then religious language and imagery is no longer assured of the determinate reality of something that it stands upon and engages with. Religious faith becomes free-floating, dissociated and uncertain of how it connects with practice. It may begin to look very like *fantasy*. Hence the uncertain status of religious ideas and symbols in postmodernity: deconstructed and disseminated, they are ubiquitous but unattached. They remain as interesting and attractive to us as ever; but they seem oddly *impotent*. It is no longer possible to be sure either what people **really believe**, or what difference faith makes to life.

It is impossible, for example, to tell whether most people 'really believe' in life after death, or not. In everyday speech we imagine the dead **up there looking down upon us**, and either watching us benignly or perhaps commenting unfavourably upon our antics. We are conscious of our own dead living on in our imaginations, and a few people are prepared to say expressly that that is the *only* afterlife that the dead have. But the great majority of people never become explicit. They are aware of the imagery of life after death, and they will occasionally themselves use one or another of the many stock phrases in which we preserve a memory of the old eschatology:

he's gone to meet his Maker
till kingdom come
he deserves to rot in hell
it's not the end of the world
I like to think of them up there, looking down on me

But most people never become more explicit than that, because we live in a time when **real belief**, either way, is simply out of date. Out of date, certainly, for us in the West. We quite often hear people say, with a touch, but no more than a touch, of envy that in the Muslim world people still **really believe** in God – but even that may be something of an overstatement, because in the Muslim world there are already very large numbers of lapsed believers, ironized believers, and believers in whom the skin by means of which realistic faith protects itself from contamination has become stretched very, very thin. The Muslim world has not been able entirely to insulate itself from the slow process of attrition, by Marxism, by 'Americanism', and now by postmodernity. In postmodernity we know all the symbolism better than ever, but symbols don't have referents that are ontologically independent of them, and there isn't a stable and agreed real order of things out there, any more. Old-style dogmatic faith doesn't make sense, and old-style dogmatic unbelief is equally off-beam. Nor, of course, are we 'agnostics': theism, atheism and agnosticism are *all* of them wrong, because the very notion of **having a position** is obsolete. Where there is no solid ground any more, nobody can take a firm stand. Rather, our situation in postmodernity is like that of the novelist in whose hospitable imagination anything and everything is readily *enter-*

tained, but **real belief** has no place, because there is nothing for it to latch on to.

We all of us *entertain* religious ideas and symbols, but their bearing upon practice has become very uncertain. In the West a generation ago social psychologists often remarked that they were not able to find any way in which 'the religious' comprised a distinct group in the population. Roman Catholics were the last Christians to comprise something like a distinct social group; but nowadays they too blend into the general population along with Protestants and Jews. Amongst Christians and Jews, at least, religious faith is usually privatized to the point of invisibility. (Muslims still strive to maintain their own visibly distinct identity, but we do not know how many generations it will last.)

Furthermore, in many contexts – and especially in one's public and working life – political correctness (or professional ethics) now requires and commands us to keep our own personal views out of it. Thus a solicitor or a general medical practitioner, in her daily work, is required *not* to obtrude upon her clients her own personal views about questions of religion, morality or politics. A professional is expected to be a very self-effacing kind of adviser. And, rather similarly, politicians who hold the very highest public office are nowadays careful – as J. F. Kennedy was – to let it be known that their personal religious allegiance does not and will not obtrude upon and prejudice their performance of their public duties.

It is a paradox rarely discussed that the preacher in church freely urges the congregation to act out their faith in daily life, without ever mentioning or even noticing the inconvenient fact that in public and working life it is usually a moral duty *not* to do so. Social convention requires a rather high degree of privatization and concealment of religious belief and practice. Such things are talked about in public only by religious professionals, or in contexts where those attending know what to expect. Otherwise, they are a matter for consenting adults in private.

If then in postmodernity religious language and symbols are ubiquitous in the culture in dissociated form, whilst personal faith is privatized to the point of invisibility (and, for reasons of political correctness, is no longer *allowed* to make much practical difference to life anyway), it is not surprising that in recent generations theology has been running close to fantasy literature.

The sources of modern fantasy literature in the West are various: they include travellers' tales from the later Middle Ages onwards; speculations about 'the plurality of worlds' in the seventeenth century, giving rise eventually to modern science fiction; Gothic revivalism, from the late eighteenth century up to modern 'swords and sorcery' cinema; and folklore, fairy tale and children's literature from the early nineteenth century onwards. No doubt the common theme is an intense nostalgia for childhood, for enchantment, and for the old pre-scientific world-view. Fantasy literature is counter-cultural protest, and an attempt to preserve an old way of thinking *despite* its inability to connect with the modern world.

In England, growing out of High-Victorian religious medievalism, there has been a tradition of Christian fantasy-writing. Amongst those who have contributed to it are George Macdonald, G. K. Chesterton, David Lyndesay, Arthur Machen, Charles Williams, J. R. R. Tolkien and C. S. Lewis. Many other names might be mentioned, but the world-wide popularity of Lewis's Narnia books is very striking. Their use of the fantasy form shows *both* how impossible to us 'straight' and non-ironical supernatural belief has already become, *and also* how intensely we still want our children to know about it, and to have been exposed to it. This entire world of thought is stone dead, but it made us what we are, its relics are all around us, and if we were wholly to lose touch with it we fear that we would risk losing our very souls. So it seems, and so the English – and some other peoples too, perhaps – cling tenaciously to their own post-Christianity. Their poet is Geoffrey Hill, the archetypal fiercely-Christian post-Christian who knows it's dead but in whom it will *not* lie down. He represents the very last, *post-mortem*, stage in the old great tradition of Anglican poetry. In Eliot, it was all still sort-of-true, but only in an Oriental-mystical and non-realistic kind of a way; in Andrew Young, it might still turn out to be true after death; in Betjeman, you can go on feeling that it might all be true so long as one can go on believing in the superior wisdom of the child within one; in R. S. Thomas, one grits one's teeth in a somewhat-embittered silence; and now in Hill one bears witness to what has been lost by the energy with which one berates one's contemporaries on its behalf. One goes down fighting, in the beloved lost cause.

A similar mood has recently appeared in the new highly-reactive Right Postmodernist and neo-conservative theologians. Their leader, John Milbank, echoes C. S. Lewis's Cambridge Inaugural Lecture in the way he portrays himself as obstinately and almost single-handedly struggling to keep alive in writing a tradition that has died out in 'the real world' of practice. The church may be dead, but the theologian battles to give it at least a literary afterlife. He is writing the theology of a church that doesn't exist but which, he thinks, *ought* to exist. He is a theological Geoffrey Hill.

Why? Milbank says that he must hope that 'his merely theoretical continuation of the tradition will open a space' within which 'a true practical repetition' of Christianity may perhaps one day occur.[1] But this is, frankly, not imaginable, and I am suggesting in this little group of books about 'ordinary-language theology' that we would do better to admit that the old Western ecclesiastical theology is some two or three centuries past its sell-by date. We should give up nostalgic British fantasy-theology. Instead of living in denial and trying to recreate a lost world, we would do better to spend our time in trying to discover our present actual religious situation by studying ordinary language. With luck this will remind us to ask ourselves what, in any case, we were expecting. Did we suppose that the church, its moral teachings and its doctrines were somehow eternal and indestructible? The old Latin theology *itself* did not regard ecclesiastical Christianity as the last stage in the historical development of the Christian tradition. On the contrary, the church readily confessed itself to be just a holding operation, a transitional stage to be compared with the wilderness wandering of ancient Israel. And if the church has now completed its historical task, then we should *not* be trying to prolong the life of the old theology; we should be looking out for the signs of the long-awaited post-ecclesiastical age. The tradition called it the promised land, the saints' rest, the millennium, the kingdom of God. It was to be radically post-historical, post-ecclesiastical, post-dogmatic, post-patriarchal, and (by the way) globalized – just as we are, in postmodernity. Perhaps we should give up our destructive love-affair with an irrecoverable past, and instead learn to love the present.

6

The World at the End of the World

One of the most important and influential ideas in the whole Judaeo-Christian tradition has been the idea of a post-historical world at the end of the world, a new age of universal freedom and reconciliation in which all the various painful oppositions and tensions that at present characterize the human condition have been finally overcome.

This new age has had many names: **'that day', 'those days', the day of Yahweh, the New Jerusalem, the messianic age, the world to come, the kingdom of God, the kingdom of heaven, the millennium, the rest of the saints, 'over Jordan', the promised land, Zion** and many, many more. It is **the American Dream, the New World**, a social hope that is both religious and political. It is invoked just as vividly by Martin Luther King and John Lennon as it was earlier by Hegel, Marx and the socialist and anarchist traditions between the mid-eighteenth and the mid-twentieth centuries. It underlies all our utopias, just as Plato's *Republic* seems to underlie all our cacotopias.[1]

In the West the hope of this better world in the future was the consolation of the oppressed and the motor of history. It underlay all forms of the belief in progress and still figures in the thought of prominent contemporary philosophers such as Jürgen Habermas and John Rawls, where it functions as a Kantian 'regulative ideal' – the idea of a perfectly just or a perfectly and transparently communicative society, which is used as a standard by which to test current moral and political situations and policies. It survives also in the various attempts to create fully 'mutual' economic enterprises in which every worker is a shareholder, or every customer a member, such as co-operatives, partnerships, credit unions and mutual societies.

A good early example of what was meant by the overcoming of oppositions is the contrast, still constitutive of our present experience, between the demands of the Law imposed upon us by God or society, and the wishes of the human heart. Classically, this conflict would be overcome when the law came to be written upon people's hearts,[2] so that there would no longer be any painful tension between duty and inclination. People would become morally autonomous: as mothers say, they 'wouldn't need to be told'.

In addition, the end of the contrast between the actual and the ideal would mean also the end of the contrast between this world and a better world 'beyond' it, and therefore too the end of ideology and dogmatic belief. It means the end of the contrast between our natural biological life and divine eternal life.[3] This means also the end of the historic opposition between holy God and sinful man, and with it the end of the mediated type of religion that has sought to bridge the gap between them, for in the New Jerusalem there is, as the New Testament says, 'no temple . . . and the city has no need of sun or moon to shine upon it'.[4] God is no longer localized and objectified, but dispersed, so that everything is irradiated with divinity and God is 'all in all' – 'everything in everyone'.[5] The old opposition between the sacred and the profane realms, church and state, disappears. The city's gates are never closed:[6] traffic flows freely through them all the time. There is only the one world, and every bit of it is always brightly lit. No shadows are cast in heaven. There is no night,[7] and therefore no fear, and no instrumental use of religion to gain security. The sacrificial system disappears, and prayer and worship are changed into an 'open' and non-objective cosmic gratitude, described in early Christianity as *sacrificium laudis*, the eucharist, the sacrifice of thanksgiving.

The world at the end of the world is a world after history. Instead of living in linear historical time one lives in something more like standing time, *nunc stans*. Life is still temporal, and may include various specially-fictioned times,[8] but it is no longer 'going anywhere', because we have arrived. **This is it.** So the contrast between life as we live it at present, on the march, under the law and subject to the rule of various civil and religious lords, and the rest and reward that we hope for in the *hereafter*, disappears. Law ethics is replaced by solar ethics, and social life becomes at last thoroughly democratic. When human life is no longer lived in subjection to kings, fathers, masters or any non-human powers, the world finally becomes fully humanized. As Jesus remarks in Matthew 22.30, sexuality is no longer confined within the limits of patriarchal orthodoxy. Religious meaning becomes ubiquitous, so that 'God' just equals 'Life', and the traditional last things are brought forward into present experience. In the world with no beyond, everything is ours, now. There is no longer any need to appeal or refer to anything else but this standing now – which is why the highest religious state is one of perfect non-dogmatic belieflessness. Unreservedly, one **throws oneself** into life now: there is not and cannot be any religious act greater than that. Kingdom religion is solar living.

I have described the undoing of the great oppositions in mainly religious terms, but I might equally well have described them in philosophical language, as Kierkegaard and Tillich do. The distinctions were first impressed upon Western thought by Greek philosophy in general, and by Plato in particular. They include, for example, the contrasts between Being and non-being, finite and infinite, time and eternity, Nature and Spirit, essence and existence, freedom and necessity (or law), particular and universal, and so forth. They were – perhaps from the second or third centuries BCE, at the time when Deutero-Isaiah was written – incorporated into the developing Jewish and Christian ideas of God and God's relation to the world in general and to the human being in particular. Once the whole system had been set up, the distinctions entrenched an acutely painful tension in the spiritual life: we can find our true happiness only in God, but God is so far above us as to be incomprehensible. Christ's work was, paradoxically, to bridge the oppositions without dissolving them away. The Church of Christ mediated his saving work to us through the sacraments, but final redemption was deferred to the end of time. So in orthodox church-Christianity God remains unknowable and Christ's work remains less-than-fully-effective so long as this life lasts.

An excellent one-sentence summary of the contents of the New Testament declares that 'Jesus preached the kingdom; but it was the church that came'. There is a very sharp sense of let-down near the beginning of Christianity. Jesus preached the imminent arrival of the world at the end of the world, and its leading features are faithfully reported in our surviving, though somewhat corrupted, traditions of his teaching. But the coming of the kingdom was delayed, and by the end of the apostolic age the emergent Gentile church was developing into one more 'historical' system of social and religious control, the church militant, with the sacramentally-mediated grace and the absolute government by a college of high priests (or bench of bishops) that remains familiar to us today.

Today, the disciplinary control of the church over matters of faith and morals has weakened so much that we have largely forgotten how cruel and repressive it formerly was, and how ardently people cherished the hope of a better order beyond it. But what seems to have happened is that deep changes in the culture – not only better study of the Bible, but also the turn to this world, and the rise of critical thinking and of liberal democracy in politics – these changes have been over a long period steadily dismantling the great oppositions around and upon which Western culture was built. They have led to the death of God and the spiralling decline of the church, and people have concluded that Christianity must be almost over. They have not considered the other possibility, that the development of Christianity is still unfolding, and what we are now witnessing is a change of dispensation, as the church's own inner logic brings it to an end, and Christianity takes on its long-awaited post-ecclesiastical form.

Remember, the great distinctions and oppositions around which Western philosophy and Western religion developed are all of them human constructs, which reflect the historical situation in which they arose. The key ideas have to do with authority and the control of life by the Law, and with an ethic of deferred satisfactions; and in their day they made a lot of sense (at least, if you agreed that the world at the end of the world was not yet a practical possibility). But all ideas – even moral and philosophical ideas – have a limited lifespan, and what one generation of human beings have built, another and later generation may dismantle. What history did, history can undo again. Just as British colonialists in the nineteenth century took overseas with them moral, political and legal ideas which were eventually to bring about the downfall of the British Empire, so ecclesiastical Christianity, in its foundation documents and in its own apologia for itself, always harboured ideas that were eventually to lead to the supersession of the church.

I am not here reintroducing either the theological idea of a divine Providence that guides the course of world history through a series of 'dispensations' or any other historicist doctrine. I am saying only that the old disciplinary world-view constructed by Plato and others was in every respect *a human invention*. In its day it was so powerful and seemed to be so much needed that in early Christianity it very soon prevailed over the original gospel. As a result, the world at the end of the world, the 'kingdom', was in effect deferred till after death. But Christianity has always known in its heart that the kingdom-world was supposed to be realized on this earth. Every day we said 'Thy kingdom come on earth', and Christianity has always known that it falls short *by a whole dispensation* of what was promised at its launch. It has hardly ever yet been anywhere near to what it should be. It has for the most part hitherto been the religion of the Grand Inquisitor and not the religion of Jesus, for reasons which the Grand Inquisitor states very clearly.

Now, however, we live in an epoch when historical developments have progressively deconstructed the old disciplinary world-view. These developments include the world-wide triumph of liberal democratic politics and the decline of every sort of ideological politics, together with general acceptance of a strong doctrine of individual human rights. Nobody sees 'beyond' these ideas, and they bring us to the end of history – in the sense that democracy is *itself* an endless conversation, and a continuous process of adaptation to change that never evolves beyond itself. The democratic process is an historical achievement that *has* no 'beyond': it just goes on, without ever needing to postulate and aspire after a further and more final stage of political development beyond itself. Fully-developed liberal democracy is already post-historical. Liberal democracy is kingdom-politics; it is end-of-the-world politics, and it is profoundly post-ecclesiastical.

The second development to be mentioned is that in just the last two generations we have come to live in a fully-technological and globalized world, which is intensely and continuously communicative. Rapid technological advance has made for a much better balance of power between the human and non-human realms, and the globalization of humanity's conversation with itself undermines all local 'absolutes' and power-structures. The whole globe is becoming democratized: it is becoming a theatre and a market that never shuts, in which anything goes and upon which everything floats.

And the third development is the development of critical thinking itself. The story here is very well-known, and I mention only its most recent effect: in the end it demythologizes everything. It de-programmes us, making us into highly-reflexive, highly self-conscious people who can entertain everything but who cannot 'really believe' anything – in a word, postmodern and post-dogmatic people. I have said this before and I say it again: there is no longer any possibility of authentic, non-ironical, 'straight' dogmatic belief in one local ideology, and the phrase 'critical realism', used by some sadly unreflective persons, is an oxymoron.

I am not to be understood as simply equating postmodernity with the kingdom of God. But I am saying that we have come to an historical epoch in which theologians should turn their attention away from ecclesiastical theology, which is a lost cause, and towards something more like kingdom theology, which is a kind of religious writing that is appropriate after God, after the church, and after ideology, in an age that has become post-historical, radically humanistic, and highly conscious and communicative.

7

Passing Out

The word **humanitarian** is highly postmodern. Everyone must have noticed how much it has come to be used and overused in the last two decades – perhaps because it functions as a password. By using it we remind ourselves of how different we are from the people of earlier generations. Whatever our other faults (and they are many), this at least is something very precious that is distinctive of our tradition, and to study its history is to gain a clear insight into the character of postmodernity as the last, scattered and anonymous phase in the historical development of Christianity.

'Humanitarianism' began life as a technical term in theology, but very late – only in the early nineteenth century.[1] Before we discuss it, something needs first to be said about the older tradition, namely that it was very much less humanistic than might have been expected. In first-millennium Christianity you might find examples (though not very many) of people commending, and even performing, some of the traditional seven 'corporal works of mercy': feeding the hungry, giving drink to the thirsty, clothing the naked, harbouring the stranger, visiting the sick and prisoners, and burying the dead. But what made these acts commendable was not their being done out of straightforward love and pity for a fellow-human in need, but their being done in obedience to the command of Christ (Matthew 25.35), in imitation of his example, and for the sake of one's own salvation. First-millennium Christianity was, overwhelmingly, about the search for salvation: it was *not* about the love of one's neighbour.[2] The religiously-serious person did not move *towards* the neighbour, but *away* from him. The neighbour was 'the world':

the neighbour was to be fled. The idea that the contemplation of great human need and suffering should arouse an intense love and pity which is religiously edifying and morally galvanizing is very recent. The older outlook regarded the rank-ordering of society as expressing a value scale. People of higher rank were 'a better class of person', who lived in 'a better area' and were more suitable company for one's children. They were 'the quality'. Conversely, in a world where everything was seen as ordained by God, the misery of the poorest was presumed to be their deserved fate. They lived in 'the worst slums' and 'dens of vice'. Social action to improve their condition seemed quite uncalled-for. One is reminded of the fact that when in the sixteenth century mass unemployment first appeared in the major towns of Western Europe the reaction of the authorities was not to pity the unemployed and try to help them, but to blame them for being idle vagabonds and to punish them.[3] Severely – for they were whipped, loaded on to carts, taken far out of the city and then abandoned. Our tradition was not humanistic. One might say that in England it had fully and finally become so only *after* people had ceased to distinguish between the 'deserving' and the 'undeserving' poor – which means that we are talking about a date well into the twentieth century.

When did our humanism first begin? It began in the Middle Ages, with the Litanies of the Passion and with the production after about 1065 of representations of the crucifixion which contort Christ's body so as to oblige the viewer to feel how much he suffers.[4] It began with the cult of the Precious Blood and the Sacred Heart of Jesus. It began with Ailred of Rievaulx's *amor carnalis Christi* (love of Christ's flesh) and his warm belief that human love and intimate friendship are not a threat or a temptation but a stepping-stone to divine love.[5] In a word, our humanism began at the moment in Western history when the focus of devotional attention began to shift from God to the suffering of a fellow-human being. The leading figures were to be found amongst the early Franciscans and the early Cistercians.

For a long period in second-millennium Christianity, then – perhaps from 1065 to 1914 – love and pity for the Crucified might prompt a person also to feel love and pity for the needy and suffering fellow-human. But this humanism was in various ways conditional or limited. You might indeed make provision in your will for the endowment of almshouses, schools, hospitals and charitable distributions, but your motive in the fifteenth century was likely to be your own salvation and your posthumous good reputation. Your bedesmen were expected in perpetuity to pray for and to commemorate their munificent Foundress. And right up to the twentieth century, and for so long as people believed in a moral Providence in the world, the suspicion persisted that a good and just God wouldn't have allowed a person to get into such a wretched plight unless he thoroughly deserved it. So the most self-consciously 'orthodox' Protestants are likely to have a highly *anti*-humanitarian attitude to AIDS victims even to this day. Indeed, they make no bones about regarding 'liberals' and 'humanists' as proponents of an alien ideology. They are proud of their own inhumanity: it is orthodox.

For most of Christian history nobody thought that the state had any responsibility to ascertain or capacity to ameliorate what in 1900 would have been called 'the condition of the people'. Only very gradually after the Enlightenment did the state begin to count the population, to treat at least a minimal care of the poor as a charge upon the parish, and to assume some responsibility for education, health and family welfare. But even as late as 1900 **humanitarian** was still a dirty word. Only in the later twentieth century did humanitarian considerations come to play a large part in political discourse, and only in the last years of the millennium did states first seriously think of going to war for humanitarian reasons.

The first lesson from all this is that people are not 'naturally' humane or humanitarian at all. They have become so only as the result of a very long and complex process of historical development which occupied in effect the whole of the second Christian millennium in the West. Gradually, and *via* the figure of Christ, people began to think that a human body – not an idealized godlike human body, but an ordinary human body – is a proper object of specifically religious attention; that the ordinary human emotions that we feel when contemplating the body – and especially bodily suffering – can be taken up into religion and into moral resolution;[6] and finally that 'humanitarian concern', feeling aroused by particular cases of human suffering, can be a morally-sufficient reason for costly personal and political action, and even for going to war.

Interestingly, the kind of humanism that inspired the foundation and the growth of the Red Cross in Switzerland in 1863, and of the great humanitarian charities after World War Two, is centrally and specifically Christian in origin. It derives from early-twelfth-century feeling for the Crucified Jesus. But it could come to its fullest and clearest expression only *after* the death of God, and therefore the end of the idea that the afflicted must surely deserve the suffering that they endure. Only after the death of God can we fully appreciate the religious significance of Christ's passion. Thus historic ecclesiastical Christianity reveals its own transitional character. Its inner logic is fulfilled only when it passes out into the age that succeeds it, an age in which a certain diffused religiosity is ubiquitous, but in which clear religious labels and disjunctions of the old 'orthodox' kind are no longer morally acceptable. So historic ecclesiastical Christianity has to die in order to complete its own mission.

It is to be noted that other religious traditions – even those most closely related to Christianity – have not shown the same impulse to self-transcendence. On the contrary, we rather take it for granted that Jewish charitable endeavours shall be devoted to Jewish objects, and that the philanthropic concern of Muslim countries is directed towards the welfare of fellow-Muslims elsewhere. There are a few exceptions which should be mentioned: members of the Saudi royal family are occasionally reported as giving charitable donations to non-Muslim persons or causes, and in Israel there is an organization, Rabbis for Human Rights, which is very honourably concerned about the welfare of Palestinians. But the general point stands: for about four decades in the Christian or post-Christian West, *and there alone*, it has been almost a cliché, and a very significant cliché, that needy people should be helped **irrespective of race, colour**

or creed. In brief, whereas 'historical' religion says that it is most important to discriminate (between us and them, the virtuous and the wicked, the orthodox and the heretic, etc.), for post-modern humanitarianism, thoroughgoing anti-discrimination is axiomatic. The traditional religious concern for the self, the soundness of its beliefs and the purity of its motives, has vanished. No consideration whatever is morally relevant except the other's need for food, for shelter, or for medical treatment. At the time of writing, the British public are expressing themselves willing to go to war on behalf of the displaced Albanian Kosovars, and hardly anybody in the West even thinks of the fact that we are talking about fighting on behalf of Muslims against fellow-Christians. It isn't relevant. Evidently, just in the past few years we have left behind the ecclesiastical kind of Christianity with its jealous claim to exclusive and total allegiance, and its peculiar grip on the self. We have transcended it, or it is in process of transcending itself, into something greater, more anonymous and universal; and no other religion has yet transcended itself in quite this way.[7] No other religion has a philosophy of history that leads it to *expect* its own self-transcendence at the end of time.

We turn now to the curious history of the word **humanitarian.** Its earliest uses, in the period around 1820 to 1840, were not ethical *at all*. They described certain doctrinal positions. A humanitarian was a person such as a Unitarian, who affirmed the humanity but denied the divinity of Christ. Alternatively a humanitarian was a theological *anthropomorphite*, a word that has been in use since antiquity to describe the sort of person who might be misled by Michelangelo's frescoes into supposing that God the Father has a human form. In our own post-philosophical age many people do seem to think of God as a very, very large human being. And thirdly, the term humanitarian might describe the sort of person who, like Karl Marx, thinks that 'man is the highest being for man': the only proper religious object for us is the concrete universal humanity, symbolized in Auguste Comte's religion of humanity by the figure of a mother and child.

All these three theological meanings of 'humanitarian' reflect the Enlightenment concern to reconstruct all knowledge as a human creation and from the human point of view, a project which naturally prompts the thought that if the proper *study* of mankind is man, perhaps the proper scope of our *moral duty* should correspondingly be restricted to the human realm. And if we are always within the human realm and see everything from the human point of view – if indeed the encompassing reality within which we live and move and have our being is simply our own human 'species-being' – then perhaps for each of us the *religious object* too should be seen simply as humanity. And in suggesting this Ludwig Feuerbach and Karl Marx were continuing the Enlightenment project into the 1840s.

There is another reason why **humanity** was popular in the 1840s: from an early-feminist standpoint it was more inclusive than older terms such as 'manhood' and 'mankind'. Thus the liberal Anglican preacher F. W. Robertson of Brighton pointedly and for feminist reasons stopped speaking of the *manhood* of Christ and instead always used the phrase 'the humanity of Christ'. From about 1850 other religious liberals begin regularly to argue that if we can be moved by the figure of the Crucified to love and pity and to a desire to give our lives to his service, why should we not be similarly moved by the plight of the poorest in our great manufacturing towns, the needy whom he calls his brothers and sisters?

Thus theology is translated into anthropology, and religious doctrine into an ethical crusade. From about 1850 a humanitarian is a philanthropist, a lover of mankind and a 'bleeding-heart liberal', or 'do-gooder' – because (as the OED volume, s.v., 1901, points out) use of the word humanitarian was for a long period 'nearly always contemptuous'. Right up to the eve of the First World War the older view remained dominant. As Martineau put it in 1858, 'the first humanizer of mankind was their worship'; and the best and most direct way to do something about the condition of the poor was to build churches for them. Their problems were chiefly *moral*, and only the influence of religion could secure their moral improvement. Until that had been gained, charitable endeavours and political campaigning were of little use. Even as late as the 1950s, when I was ordained and went to serve my 'title' in a Northern working-class town, it was still generally supposed by the middle classes that there was a very high level of sin and darkness amongst the urban poor, who were therefore in extra need of the ministrations of clergymen. So I was assured, believe me, at length: it is not easy now to recall how deeply people used to believe in the moral and religious superiority of the 'classes' to the 'masses'.

For almost a hundred years, then, ethical humanitarianism was on the defensive. Why has everything now changed, and why has the word **humanitarian** suddenly come to be used so much?

Since the Second World War, and with the growth of the state's social provision, there has been a gradual secularization of social action. We remember now with some embarrassment the deep anger of destitute men in the 1920s who were obliged to take part in religious worship in order to get food at soup kitchens, and the resentment of poor women who were patronized by **my Lady Bountiful.** Nowadays most social action is undertaken, not by condescending amateurs, but by paid professionals who are guided by codes of practice. This has secularized the relation between benefactor and beneficiary into the relation between professional and client, and in the process a moral transformation has occurred. By the former standards, the modern professional eliminates the self to a more-than-Buddhist degree. One has to be completely cool and client-centred, eliminating any consideration of or concern for one's own feelings, motives, beliefs or opinions. One must never obtrude oneself. Today, the kind of person who is ethically most admirable is an *unperson*, a person without what everyday speech calls an 'identity': he's a soldier in a blue beret on peace-keeping duties, a person working for *Médecins sans Frontières*, a professional negotiator, or an 'aid worker'. And it is this cool, beliefless, identityless and very postmodern sort of saint who has made the word **humanitarian** respectable at last.

Most of the great humanitarian charities were originally

religious foundations, and their notion of social action was at first of the old type. You were conscious of your own religious identity and motivation; you wore your heart on your sleeve; your action was *labelled*. But they too have changed. People who 'do good' for a living do not wish to carry advertising. They want anonymity and ordinariness; they want their action to be unlabelled. Overt commitment to an ideology and an institution, as a ground of moral action, has somehow become repugnant to *all* of us. We don't like what Derrida called the 'violence' of the old distinctions: anti-discrimination in morality is the equivalent of post-structuralism in metaphysics. Doesn't every person who is stuck with a uniform and a label now yearn for beliefless, anonymous ordinariness? We would all of us prefer to wear plain clothes.

The postmodern demand for impersonality and anonymity in ethics may be compared with Jesus' teaching that one should pray, fast, and give alms 'in secret', and with Wittgenstein's conviction that 'the ethical' is somehow off the page and not clearly expressible in language. But it is a large part of what nowadays makes the best Christian not the church member, and certainly not the professional Christian, but the anonymous, post-dogmatic Christian who lies low, and keeps out of sight.

8

Is Anything Still Sacred?

Early in the twentieth century Emile Durkheim laid down the principle that religion everywhere rests upon the distinction between the sacred and the profane:

> All known religious beliefs, whether simple or complex, present one common characteristic: they presuppose a classification of all the things, real and ideal, of which men think, into two classes or opposed groups, generally designated by two distinct terms which are translated well enough by the words *profane* and *sacred* (*profane, sacré*). This division of the world into two domains, the one containing all that is sacred, the other all that is profane, is the distinctive trait of religious thought . . .

and, at the end of the same chapter, he arrives at his definition of religion:

> Thus we arrive at the following definition: *A religion is a unified system of beliefs and practices relative to sacred things, that is to say, things set apart and forbidden – beliefs and practices which unite into one single moral community called a Church, all those who adhere to them.* The second element which thus finds a place in our definition is no less essential than the first; for by showing that the idea of religion is inseparable from that of the Church, it makes it clear that religion should be an eminently collective thing.[1]

Here Durkheim is stressing that the line between things sacred and things profane is drawn not by the individual, but by society: religion is always *social.*

From the same period in the early twentieth century comes Rudolf Otto's book *The Idea of the Holy* (1917), which introduced the thesis that the concept of the holy, as a *mysterium tremendum et fascinans*, is an *a priori* category of the human mind. In itself it is non-rational, but it is activated by certain operations of reason. Thus Kant reports that he was moved to sacred awe by 'the starry heavens above and the moral law within'.

These two writers, Durkheim and Otto, express well the view, still widespread in their period, that humans are religious animals, that everybody knows what religion is, that everyone can experience sacred awe and dread and can recognize that experience as religious, and that everyone understands the religious concern to acknowledge the sacred and to draw a clear line between it and the profane. To ask what somebody's religion is, is to ask what he and his people hold sacred.

Let us pause a moment and consider the words. In Latin the old word for holy was *sacer*, from which come *sacré* (made holy, in French), and sacred or consecrated in English. When the holy has been recognized as such, it is 'defined' or fenced off in order to keep it inviolate, and this fence is what was originally called a fane, *fanum*. The profane is what lies outside the fence, in the common world. As for the fane, the enclosure that houses and protects the sacred, it has taken many forms: in ancient Israel it was reportedly at one time just a tent, whereas amongst us the word has since the late Middle Ages denoted a major shrine or temple, or other large religious building.

Until recently – perhaps until as recently as the 1960s – these ideas held. The presumption was that for every human being, as for every human society, **some things are sacred** – 'sacred' meaning set apart, cherished to the highest degree, inviolable, non-negotiable and, in particular, having to do with God and religion. There were a fair number of well-established idioms which showed the continuing prominence of the idea of the sacred in Christianity: **'Sacred to the memory of . . .'**, **sacred**

music, sacred scriptures, sacred mysteries (the eucharist), **sacred ministers** (the officiants at a celebration), and so on.

One exception to this: there was a French use of *sacré* to mean outrageous, notorious or confounded, as in the phrases *un sacré menteur* and *un monstre sacré*, used perhaps of a great figure like Picasso who has lived to become an institution, and is so far-out as to be beyond criticism.

Otherwise, we may stay with the view that until about 1960 the meaning of the sacred, the propriety of respecting the sacred by drawing a clear line between it and the profane, and the Christian use of the term were all of them unproblematic. They defined religion.

Now consider the situation today. There are only a very few sacred-idioms left in today's English, and they are all jocular or ironical:

Is nothing sacred?
a sacred cow
the sacred turf (at a big football ground)

Probably the nearest we get to a fully-serious use of the old vocabulary of the sacred is in connection with human life and human rights, which ought to be **respected as sacred**, and not **violated**. There is a whole sentence, often heard, declaring that **I believe that all life is sacred**. Otherwise, the word sacred has simply lost its force. So has the word **holy**, which is nowadays used very lightly, and in association with words like **terror, cow, mackerel, smoke, Rollers, Joe** and **City**. When they walk into **a holy place**, people no longer feel the old awe and dread at all. They are just visiting a tourist attraction, because in postmodernity the holy has been taken over *en bloc* by the heritage industry. No 'straight' holiness remains.

In what was planned to be his final synthesis, Mircea Eliade promised to discuss what he called 'the sole, but important, religious creation of the modern world. I refer to the ultimate stage of desacralization . . . it illustrates the complete camouflage of the "sacred" – more precisely, its identification with the "profane".'[2] Here Eliade refers to the feature of postmodernity that we have been discussing throughout: in recent years the old line between the sacred and the profane has disappeared, and the old intense concentration of the sacred at certain sites has become melted-down and scattered widely across the whole face of language.

Some of the old grand idioms are still remembered – for example,

The Holy Bible
Holy Communion
The Holy Name
Holy Night, Holy Week, Holy Saturday
The Holy Father
Holy Island
Holy, Holy, Holy (the Trisagion, the Sanctus)
The Holy of Holies

But nowadays, expressions such as **holy of holies, sanctum** and **sanctuary** are used very much more often in an extended, ironical, metaphorical sense to signify for example an individual's private place of refuge, than in their old weighty sense. And the same is true, as everyone has noticed, of the words **awful, awesome, dreadful, horrible, terrible, fearful** and **fearsome**. And **absolute? Absolutely!**

Thus, when in church we hear Genesis 28 being read, we may hear Jacob saying, **How dreadful is this place!**, and so be reminded of the now-archaic serious meaning of *dreadful*. But when we hear one of our contemporaries use the same expression, and say, **What a dreadful place this is!**, we are reminded of how completely the old, *serious* meanings of words like *holy*, *sacred* and *dreadful* have now vanished from everyday speech. The *Revised Standard Version* of the Old Testament (1952) tried *awesome* instead of *dreadful* at Genesis 28.11, but it is a poor substitute. In everyday speech nowadays *awesome* may still approach *sublime*: it may signify *breathtaking* or *deeply impressive*. But it is *not* used to express sacred awe of the old, grand *religious* sort. Rather similarly, some of the followers of Rudolf Otto have made a great effort to establish *numinous* in the language, as a fresh and undebased word for that which arouses awe and dread. But they failed, as the *New ODE* shows.[3] About the only things we call *numinous* are megaliths – things vague, old and moody.

In its great days, the numinous was far more than just romantically moody. It was the supernatural, and it truly terrified people. A trace of it survived until not very long ago: I recall in about 1960 meeting many people who were too frightened to enter a church building, and others who could not reach the church anyway, because they dared not walk through the graveyard that surrounded it. In the late 1960s I twice sat through the night in a 'haunted' room, by way of trying to dispel the fears of a frightened householder. But these little anecdotes remind me that I no longer hear of such superstitious terrors. Ghosts are seldom heard of now. In connection with graveyards and churches we hear about tourism and about looting and vandalism, but not about the old extreme dread. We often meet people who are very afraid of death; but we do not encounter the old drop-dead fear of God (**drop dead** *itself*, serious in the Bible,[4] is now a jocular phrase, as when we speak of someone as **drop-dead gorgeous**).

From the evidence of everyday speech, then, we are entitled to conclude that the old vocabulary of the sacred and the great distinction between the sacred and the profane realms, which at the beginning of the twentieth century still seemed to notable scholars to be constitutive of religion, had by the later years of the century simply vanished. As defined by Durkheim and Otto, religion must have suddenly ceased to exist. The old vocabulary may still be used in certain sub-worlds such as the church, but in ordinary life and everyday speech it is lost. Postmodernity has deconstructed, ironized and scattered all of the old religious meanings. The words are still heard; indeed, they are ubiquitous. But they don't have and cannot have their old, grand force. There remains a loose and general sense in which everything is holy, or in which anything may suddenly strike us as holy; but the old highly-*specific* sacred is gone.

Salman Rushdie considered the issues here in his 1990

Herbert Read Memorial Lecture, **Is Nothing Sacred?**[5] As one might have expected, the lecture is a defence of imaginative literature against its army of religious critics. Rushdie describes himself as a post-religious or post-godly person who wants to be able to write freely about religious questions:

> . . . one reason for my attempt to develop a form of fiction in which the miraculous might co-exist with the mundane was precisely my acceptance that notions of the sacred and the profane both needed to be explored, as far as possible without pre-judgment, in any honest literary portrait of the way we are.
>
> That is to say: the most secular of authors ought to be capable of presenting a sympathetic portrait of a devout believer. Or, to put it another way: I had never felt the need to totemize my lack of belief, and so make it something to go to war about.[6]

Perhaps like André Gide, Rushdie sees the imaginative writer as an uncommitted artist, whose work opens a broad space in which many different points of view, different faiths and vocabularies, different affirmations and denials can come into conversation with each other. Quoting Carlos Fuentes, he asks:

> *Can the religious mentality survive outside of religious dogma and hierarchy?* Which is to say: Can art be the third principle that mediates between the material and spiritual worlds; might it, by swallowing both worlds, offer us something new – something that might even be called a secular definition of transcendence?
>
> *I believe it can.* I believe it must.[7]

So for Rushdie literature has a special, mediating function in the culture:

> Literature is the one place in any society where, within the secrecy of our own heads, we can hear *voices talking about*

> *everything in every possible way*. The reason for ensuring that that privileged arena is preserved is not that writers want the absolute freedom to say and do whatever they please . . . It is that we, all of us, . . . need that little unimportant room. We do not need to call it sacred, but we do need to remember that it is necessary.[8]

In the end, Rushdie wants to avoid sacralizing literature. But he does make the writer sound a little like a shaman, through whose mouth many strange voices are heard speaking. And he, like Flaubert, leaves us wondering about the position of the writer himself as human being. How, in a story like *A Simple Heart*,[9] does Flaubert combine his deep and pure sympathy for naïve faith with his equally pure and complete ironical detachment? And how can that combination be *itself* a spirituality that one can live by?

At first sight the question seems unanswerable. But in Rushdie's vocabulary, Flaubert's special combination of complete sympathy with calm non-attachment (non-*irritability*) is just the 'secular kind of transcendence' that he is looking for. It is a genuinely religious mentality, the only one now possible to us in postmodernity, and the one that is now actually *required* of professional people. Think again of the special kind of anonymous, committed openness that we earlier saw as being required of an UN soldier in a blue beret on peacekeeping duties; think of *any* professional person – doctor, social worker, teacher, police officer – who works amongst stressed people in a multi-ethnic area. Think of the postmodern moral quest for an anonymous, effaced, open, beliefless, non-judgmental and receptive sort of selfhood. That is the everyday equivalent of what Rushdie asks for in the novelist: the novelist should be as generous to his characters as the professional should be to the client. The task is quietly and habitually to give to the other the fullest expressive freedom, and it is a sort of sacred calling.

As for the question, Is anything sacred? (or, Is nothing sacred?), we can now answer it by saying that the question presupposes the contrast between the sacred and profane realms.

But the whole process of things in the life-world is a continuum, 'the Fountain', and because we see no reason to divide it up in such a way, we do not regard *sacred* and *profane*, or *holy* and *common*, as descriptive terms. Rather, their use by us is expressive and poetical: using them, we respond *ad hoc* to particular things within or to the whole process of 'life'. I call something *sacred* or *holy* if it triggers the 'cosmic' response, making me feel that not just this, but *everything*, is holy. I call something *profane, mundane* or *common* if it triggers a feeling of the interconnectedness of everything, and **It all begins to make sense.**

9

Postmodern Saints: The Selfless Professional and the Solar Performer

Two very different moralities are currently praised in ordinary language, and we have already met them both. Both are non-realist and both are postmodern; but one of them seeks moral liberation by effacing the self, whereas the other seeks moral liberation by making an exhibition or show of the self. They are so different that they may be seen as a contrasting pair of *spiritualities* which have descended to us historically from the traditional ways of negation and of affirmation in theology.

The best-known literary archetype of the first morality, the selfless professional, is the much discussed 'atheist saint', Dr Bernard Rieux, in Albert Camus' novel *La Peste* (1947; ET *The Plague*, 1948). Rieux lives in a time and a place (Oran in the early 1940s, during a severe plague) where it is no longer possible for him to believe that everything adds up, makes sense, and will come out right in the end, either in the objective world or within the self. The world is neither moral nor rational, but simply anarchic and indifferent. Whatever we do, we are all losers in the end. In this extreme situation, the best way to liberation is to *forget* the self and its traditional 'infinite concern' for its own purification and its own eternal happiness, and instead to sink one's whole life into a professional ethic and a line of work that is at least honourable and relatively uncorrupt.

In popular art the typical example of such a person is the postmodern honest detective, a maverick like Philip Marlowe, still obstinately pursuing a dream of justice in a partly-or-largely corrupt force, and in a violently unjust urban society. There are no unambiguously good causes any longer, but he battles on selflessly, the last hero, winning some, losing some. He may be rather quirky and cantankerous, but he doesn't know it and doesn't care, because he is unconcerned about himself. His work, his dream is all he is.

In real life the archetype of the selfless professional surfaces from time to time – for example, in WPC Nina Mackay, who died of stab wounds in Stratford, East London, on 24 October 1997 after attempting to arrest a dangerous man. What was then said of her, and is often said of others like her, is representative:

> she was **a dedicated professional**
> **all she ever wanted was to be a police officer**
> **she lived for her work**

Of such a person it is said that **she lived for others**, and that **she was always there when you needed her**. It was perhaps because **she never thought of herself** that she tried to tackle a man armed with a knife without wearing a protective vest. And the sentiments may perhaps seem a little banal, but we hear them often, and they make a significant moral point: in a violent and disorderly society there is no unmixed goodness and no easy way to redemption. Perhaps the best that one can find to do is to forget the self and to commit one's whole life to a professional ethical code. It is at least a way of drawing a straight line in a bent world, even if the line is cut short, too early.

Other examples of the selfless professional as a type have already been quoted above, notably the UN soldier in a blue beret on peacekeeping duties and the worker in one of the helping professions who must completely forget and set aside his personal beliefs and feelings, and become entirely 'client-centred'. The more effaced and anonymous such people are, the better they do – and, perhaps, the happier they are. If we never think about ourselves, we have no time to be unhappy.

An interesting complication arises here: nowadays there are very many people who live committed to a professional ethical code that, for the present, provides them with their basic life-stance or spirituality. Then at about the age of sixty they retire – and suddenly discover that because they have for so long set aside the self and all questions of personal faith they do not know who they are or what they really believe. Deprived of the professional role that was their life, they suddenly find themselves horribly naked and at a loss. How are they to live – and to die? Some embark upon a belated but very urgent religious quest. They become seekers, casting about, but it is rather late for them to be learning an entirely new spirituality or form of life, and almost certainly far too late to learn to think like a philosopher. I have felt inclined to say to them that their former spirituality of professional self-effacement was perhaps religiously better than their present state of self-concerned 'seeking'. Have they asked themselves what they lacked then, and what they seek now?

There is another possibility, which when I first encountered it nearly twenty years ago was my first introduction to postmodernism. Then, as now, young scientist friends and colleagues went out to California to seek out the kind of laboratory equipment that British universities cannot afford. They reported their astonishment at the lifestyles of some of their very hospitable and distinguished hosts. During the week, these characters would be impeccably low-key, rational and disciplined physicists, the best in the world, but come the weekend they would change their dress and their personalities and be off to cruise the gay scene, to chant in ashrams, or zoom into the desert for festivals like today's Burning Man.

The British, being Enlightenment rationalists, were dumbfounded by this behaviour. They thought that if you were a grey 'natsci'[1] living in a semi-detached house all week, then that is what you should be at weekends too. Being Oxbridge, and therefore *well* over a century out of date, their deep metaphysical assumptions were still Platonic. The self should be a stable unified system reflecting the objective rational unity of all reality, and especially the unity of all virtues in the Good. If you are *ever* a scientist – one committed to the ideal of organized knowledge – then you are *always* a scientist, and must be one consistently. You should be always the same: grey all week and grey at the weekend.

At first I agreed with my scientist friends, and laughed at the Californians. It took me years to see that on the contrary, the Platonic assumptions were unjustified, and that the Californians were (in postmodern terms) behaving entirely rationally. Our culture and world-view simply are *not* any longer unified, or unifiable, in the Platonic way. We don't have a single cosmos any more; we have only various manmade worlds. Why *shouldn't* we learn the habit of moving back and forth between the worlds of work and leisure, negation and affirmation, the active and contemplative lives? The world-view of science, beautiful though it is, and exciting though it is to have a part in building it, is emotionally dry, and complete only on a very narrow front. It leaves out values, art, and subjectivity's profound need for self-outpouring in symbolic expression. So it is entirely understandable that high-class physicists, after a hard week in the lab being grey, should want to put on colourful clothes and become long-haired solar performers at the weekend. Why not?

So we turn to the second sort of postmodern saint, the **real trouper**, the solar performer who always puts on a **good show.**[2] The ecclesiastical Christian, the scientist and many other sorts of platonist see Reality as an intelligible system. They see the good life as a life spent seeking objective knowledge of the truth, and then in contemplating it. To a degree that in retrospect seems quite amazing, they think first and almost solely of *knowledge*. To this day it remains very hard for many people to see how utterly gratuitous – indeed, how *absurd* – are the great initial assumptions, that Reality is an intelligible system, and that the human being is somehow predesigned to find eternal happiness through contemplative knowledge of it, and in no other way. But if we can only for a moment step outside our ancient errors, we might begin to see the point of a quite different vision of the human condition and the good life.

From the 'solar' point of view a human being is a bundle of energies or 'drives', all seeking to come out into expression – *symbolic* expression, because it is the function of symbols to attract and transmute libido. Symbols turn biology into culture. Rubbing along with other people, we evolve *shared* symbols, and so the beginnings of a common language. We have an intense need to express ourselves, to communicate with others, and so gradually to build up a common *world*. We are artists, **thespians**, who long to **come out**, express ourselves, **put our oars in**, and make our contribution. *We burn to burn*. The whole notion of an introvertive spirituality of hidden inwardness is profoundly mistaken: from the 'solar' point of view a postmodern spirituality must be highly and purely extravertive or self-outing. By our self-outing we create meaning and help to build a world.

Here it is worth mentioning the very striking example of Nelson Mandela as a postmodern saint who has combined in a remarkable degree solarity and selflessness. He has lived a highly-exposed public life on the basis of iron self-discipline in the service of a single cause, achieving a uniquely high level of world-wide respect and admiration.

The critic Lionel Trilling, in his book *Sincerity and Authenticity* (1972), noted the rising influence in modern Western culture of this ethical emotivism and expressivism. The new ethical criterion is the completeness and genuineness of one's self-expression; and since Trilling's day the idioms of solar ethics have multiplied:

coming out
pride (as in **gay pride**)
demonstration (cf. *monstrance*. We used to expose the images of the gods, or divine things. Now we **come out** and show *ourselves*)
out of the closet
warpaint (= cosmetics)
I cannot live a lie
show up
a brave sight
coming clean
strutting one's stuff

doing one's own thing / saying one's piece / doing one's act
doing it my way
let it all hang out
let one's hair down
pour one's heart out
get it off one's chest
let them see what you're made of
give it all you've got / give one's all
go the whole hog
all out
put on a good show (compare **the passing show of all existence**)
the show must go on
go down with all guns blazing
my day (as in **every dog has his day** and **in my day . . .**)

The notion of the Christian as someone who is placarded, exposed, and made 'a spectacle to the world, to angels and to men' is explored in the New Testament,[3] and it is there recognized that in suffering this fate the Christian follows Christ. But Christ underwent this fate *voluntarily*, and it is noticeable that now in postmodernity many people feel a strong moral impulse to costly self-exposure in respect of matters that only a few years ago would have been kept private and concealed. Thus the Oxford literary critic John Bayley was willing to expose the dementia of his wife Iris Murdoch (in *Iris: A Memoir*, 1998) and even allowed her to be photographed. A Scandinavian Prime Minister in the same year publicly announced his own state of depression – a statement which until very recently it would have been considered politically impossible to make. Among British Prime Ministers, nobody would have thought of announcing Anthony Eden's breakdown in 1956, or Harold Wilson's early Alzheimer's in 1976. But Ronald Reagan, more recently, said a formal farewell to the American people before he succumbed to Alzheimer's.

It is now recognized that explicitness is morally upbuilding. It helps others. And the moral imperative involved can be extraordinarily strong and can demand great courage.

An extreme example is the case of the small group of youngish gay Anglican priests who **came out** almost twenty years ago – and since then have **hung in there** (or **hung on in there**) in a state of permanent limbo, professionally almost unemployable, living from hand to mouth, and yet not abandoning the church. Courageously taking a moral lead from the more excitable tabloid newspapers, the bishops announced a policy of excluding them from beneficed employment and of declining to ordain any more self-confessed 'practising' male homosexuals, which seems to remain in force. So these men of good ability are now getting well on in middle age after a life's work which has consisted of little else but **hanging in there**. Why have they endured so long? Why have they not shrugged their shoulders and turned away to seek employment in a more kindly environment?

One may reply: because they want to be accepted for what they are. They cannot give up. They believe that honesty and openness ought to be possible even in the church. They really believe in the expressivist ethic of **coming out**. But there is more to it than that: it was and is a basic principle of kingdom theology that in the world at the end of the world everything will be brought out into the open and nothing will be allowed to remain hidden.[4] That is what words like 'apocalypse' and 'revelation' *mean*. But since the Middle Ages the church authorities have without exception preferred a policy of concealment. They have concealed, for example, violations of the rule of clerical celibacy, paedophilia amongst the clergy, and (more recently) domestic violence amongst the clergy. They have always behaved as if they think that the whole church-system is a grand illusion that they have to keep up for the sake of all the little people who are taken in by it.

A true story: in her last months of life a decade ago I regularly visited at her request a Belgian-born woman of almost ninety years, a celebrated war heroine, who in middle age had come to Britain and married the best-known English liberal clergyman of his generation. He was a feminist and a pacifist, and in his time had held the highest offices in Cambridge – Vice-Chancellor,

Head of a House, Regius Professor and whatnot. But, said his widow, he was violent. It was strange to have survived the Gestapo only to be given a worse moral shock by an English liberal clergyman. Can you guess why he was violent, I asked. She replied that she had once come upon him alone and weeping, because he believed he had 'lost his faith'. That silenced me. Such is the psychological cost of the church's compulsory dogmatic tests of faith; and such, ultimately, is the cost of the old dualistic and disciplinary world-view in which the most important things, the things we live by, are hidden from our eyes, being so very deep and being deferred so very far into the future. One had to live by faith in dogmatic guarantees given to us by authority, and if faith began to fail, one felt utterly lost and violently despairing.

But postmodernity is apocalyptic: it is religious fulfilment because it is the end of history, the last state of the world. Nothing is hidden from us, nothing is deep, and there is no as-yet-unseen better world beyond all this. On the contrary, everything is brightly-lit, everything is confessed and exposed, everything is superficial and nothing is deep. All this is all there is. There is nothing behind the scenes; *there are only these scenes*. But I like *these scenes*. I love the end of mystery, I love this absolute explicitness, I love being precipitated wholly into Now. For me it is religious fulfilment, it is what we were waiting for. In everyday speech, **it's absolute heaven**.

It is comical that at this point I am in equally sharp disagreement with two figures as disparate as the late Iris Murdoch and Jean Baudrillard. A Platonist, Murdoch hated the thought of a world in which 'nothing is deep'. Baudrillard has described the state of absolute explicitness, total exposure, towards which postmodernity drives, as 'obscene'.[5] But I say this state of total exposure is the *telos*, the goal towards which the whole Bible looks forward. It is the exposure of the Crucified, it is the self-exposure of the solar performer, it is simply how things are on judgment day, and in the New Jerusalem. It's not easy, but we'd better get accustomed to it. One can learn to love it.[6]

10

Kingdom Come

Some theorists of postmodernity – J.-F. Lyotard and Francis Fukuyama in particular, though in different ways – are alleged to teach that postmodernity is the end of history in the sense of being the end of humankind's long struggle for social and political emancipation. The end of the Cold War and the almost worldwide triumph of liberal democracy, capitalism, consumerism and belief in individual human rights brings into view the end of ideology and of all ideologically-inspired collective struggles. From now on there is not much more to do than to deepen democracy by, amongst other things, improving everyone's access to communications, to the arts and culture. A picture develops of postmodernity in the long term as a paradisal age of gaming and showing off – a life of celebration lived in the Now and without any 'external' goal or *telos*. It is further pointed out that for two generations or so the glossy magazines have been purveying exactly such a lotus-eaters' lifestyle – dreamy, narcissistic, interested in nothing but appearances and pleasure, and completely apolitical and unhistorical – first to millions of women, and nowadays also to the mass of younger men. Far from being a paradisal age at the end of time, postmodernity, in the view of these critics, begins to look more like the death of man. The 'man' of the Enlightenment was a rational and self-aware subject and a free moral agent who strove for clear consciousness, for knowledge, and for the realization of ideal value in the actual world. But now in postmodernity the human being is to become a preening, self-absorbed airhead, interested only in *looking* good, and with no idea any more of what it might be to *do* good. Meanwhile outside the world of the glossy magazines history appears to go on, and the weight of human suffering appears to be as great as ever – making postmodernist theory look like little more than an ideology of denial propagated by metropolitan types in the fashion and advertising industries.

So runs the common indictment, and there's a great deal more than could be said – and *is* said, very often – along the same lines. But it is a misunderstanding; and the misunderstanding begins with the phrase 'the end of history', which has meant a number of different things to different philosophers since Hegel.

In this book, 'the end of history' is understood in (approximately) Nietzsche's sense. Until quite recently our knowledge-systems and our technologies were relatively weak, and human beings could not see themselves as having sole responsibility for making and remaking themselves and their world. On the contrary, our contribution to shaping reality seemed to be very small. We were rivalled, surrounded and threatened by a large number of monsters, aliens, spirits and other powers and forces. These rivals also invaded and weakened human subjectivity. On the larger scale, it seemed that human societies could only cohere, survive and flourish if they were governed by great divinely-accredited disciplinary institutions, of which the state and the church were the two most important. Monarchs ruled by divine right, religious institutions dispensed religious law, and religious belief-systems assured us that the world-order was established and maintained by an all-powerful God. If we kept God's law, we would survive. The harshness of life on the long march, under quasi-military discipline, was mitigated by the double promise of a blessed life after death for the faithful individual, and of a fully-humanized world at the end of time for the human race as a whole.

With the European Enlightenment came the first reasonably complete system of mathematical physics, the first attempts to state a systematic doctrine of the rights of man, and the beginnings of free trade, free expression and liberal democracy. All this could readily be seen as portending a new era in which humankind's ancient eschatological hopes would begin to be realized on earth, and Kant spoke of 'the coming-of-age of man'. Human beings would no longer be like boarding-school children. They would become fully-responsible adults. The only law that they would live under would be a law that they themselves had freely agreed and promulgated.

The idea of the end of history is a child of the Enlightenment – and, in a longer perspective, it is also a child of Christian eschatology. Thus the United States is and always has been *at once* a secular Enlightenment republic which claims to be a fulfilment of humanity's ancient hope for deliverance from the oppressive regimes of the Old World, *and also* itself the New World, a place where refugees from the religious oppression of the old world could set about building the kingdom of God on earth. Hence the USA is *both* the most secular *and* the most religious of countries, both messianic and highly multi-ethnic, a nation both entirely man-made and unusually godly. In this context extremes meet, and the most-secular coincides with the most-religious. When religion's hopes are fulfilled, religion disappears as a distinct sphere of life: there is no temple in the New Jerusalem.

Against this background we can see our own postmodernity as being not anti-Enlightenment, as some people picture it, but as Enlightenment-squared, hyperbolic Enlightenment. Towards the end of the twentieth century, 'post-realist' philosophy had developed to the point when we humans could learn to see ourselves as the only begetters of our own language, our own cultures, our own habits of perception, our own forms of consciousness, and therefore of our own world as a whole. We have evolved amongst ourselves every bit of the intelligible structure that we attribute to ourselves and to the world about us. *We* created our physics, *we* developed our biology, *we* invented our psychology. Everything around us is a communally-evolved human historical product. Together, we have made it all up.

In philosophy all this is so obvious that some people still find it hard to see, but they may be ready to recognize the huge leap forward towards systematic completeness of our scientific knowledge in the past generation or two, and the parallel leap in the power and scope of our technologies that is currently occurring. Radical humanism is becoming an obvious fact of life, and it has brought ethical humanitarianism in its train. At the same time, as human communication has come to form a world-wide web that encircles and envelops the whole terrestrial globe, even unphilosophical people may begin to grasp how human sign-systems penetrate and shape the structure of reality itself.

Thus when we speak in postmodernity of a fully-humanized world, we are talking about a major shift in the relations between culture and nature. Culture is no longer a small protected enclave in which humans huddle together, surrounded by the vast untamed and demon-haunted wilderness of nature; for nowadays culture has grown so large that it encircles, describes and protects nature. Culture *precedes* nature, for nature has no other intelligibility except that with which we have endowed it.

The end of history is simply the feeling of liberation we have when at last we are comprehensively and finally delivered from the old superstitious terrors that have hitherto always haunted human beings. The world is simply *our* world, ours and nobody else's. As a result, 'history' for us postmoderns is now no more than 'time': it just goes on. It has no special shape or direction.

Certainly there are many relics in language and in popular entertainment of the old ideas. People try to give themselves a little *frisson* by saying **The truth is out there** and **we are not alone** – but in fact everyone knows that of course it isn't, and of course we are. Psychological states reminiscent of possession can still occur, and are reflected in popular idioms:

I don't know what got into me
I don't know what's come over me
The devil's in me tonight
He played like a man possessed

– and so on: but these relics, like the relics of theological belief, are kept only for sentimental reasons. Nobody does or can take such beliefs seriously any longer.

Postmodernity then is religious fulfilment, and even the end of history, in the sense that it is thoroughgoing anti-realism, radical humanism, and ethical humanitarianism. We are no longer at the mercy of supernatural powers and forces, and no longer under discipline in the way we were, because we no longer see ourselves as *preparing* for a great event that is yet to come. We have come to the end of the idea that history *has* an end. Our continuing struggle with such enemies as racism, nationalism and oppressive moralism is a struggle against the residues of our own past that linger within ourselves. There is no external evil – we should take a non-realist view of evil – but there remains plenty of autogenic evil for us to combat. We are now our own only enemies.

Against this background we see that there is no reason for portraying postmodernity as narcissistic and indolent. On the contrary, *la lutte continue*, but now we battle not against supernatural foes but against what our own past has made of ourselves and of our world. One is reminded that the end calls for the creation of 'a new heaven and a new earth' (Isaiah 65.17; 66.22; II Peter 3.13; Revelation 21.1). In philosophical language, the reason for this is that both the world and the self are complicated collections of *habits*: habits of perception, habits of evaluation, and habits of interpretation; habits some of which are good and some bad for us. In a radically new religious situation which calls for the reimagining and remaking both of the self and of the world, there has to be a large-scale unlearning of old habits and an equally large-scale reimagining of how we and our world might be remade. Far from being frivolous and self-absorbed, the postmodern period is an age when, in the words of Elias Canetti, 'everything must be rethought'.

The process has already begun. The Human Genome Project is running ahead of schedule, and geneticists working on it and in related areas are already discussing how genetic engineering may most effectively redesign human beings in the future. Things that are already happening give some indication of what people might opt for when they have a free choice in the matter: in many parts of the world people may choose that their first child shall be a male, already leading in China to an excess of males; people who have the opportunity may wish to use genetic engineering to eliminate hereditary defect or disability in their children; Californian mothers are very ready to pay for the cosmetic surgery that will make their children look suitable for the cast of *Baywatch*. The indications are that if and when prospective parents are able to choose the characteristics they want in their children, the result may be a rather dull world with a much narrower range of human variability and no quite novel human types.

Debates like these, about how human beings and the human world are going to be re-created in the future, sound eminently theological and one might wish that theologians could become involved in them. The theoretical basis for such involvement lies in the ancient religious recognition that the human being is 'made in the image of God' and is at least the maker of the little world that is built up around the self. Thus theology has always seen an analogy of proportionality between the way God created the cosmos, the great world, and the way 'man', God's finite counterpart, creates the human life-world. Today, after the end of metaphysics and of theological realism, we no longer have either a ready-made cosmos out there or an objective Creator out there. There is only Be-ing and language, out of which humans and the human world are constructed. But the theological character of the relationship between humans and the human life-world remains, and now that our technology is becoming so powerful that it invites us to contemplate reinventing both ourselves and our world, we need theological thinking to show how to set about **playing God**. In popular speech the stock phrase about 'playing God' is often introduced as if with the aim of calling a halt: but we are *already* **playing God**, and in the future will be doing so more and more. We need theological thinking to help ourselves imagine how to build a world that looks as if it has been made by Love – because it is indeed our world-love that differentiates and builds up the world. Do you see? – people used to think that the world looked as if it had been made by Love because, they supposed, a loving God had made it. Now we should put it rather differently: so far as it is indeed lovely, our world reflects the human world-love that built it. We look at our homeland and we look at skies, water, birds and insects with the eyes of generations of farmers, painters, country parsons, naturalists and others. They gave us the vocabulary through which we see it all.

Hitherto theology has been ecclesiastical theology: tradition-orientated, it investigates, articulates and defends the doctrinal and moral teaching of the church. But in this little series of books I have been arguing that in our everyday speech Christianity is already moving into its post-ecclesiastical phase. The church is no longer of the first importance to religion. It is too small and weak, has slipped too far downmarket, and is ethically too far behind current secular standards (as is shown when, for example, it battles to get itself exempted from international human rights legislation). There no doubt continues to be a place for the church, but it no longer has the authority to command theology to dance to its tune. In the larger world the Spirit – or perhaps the *Zeitgeist* – has moved on, and we should now be writing not ecclesiastical theology, but what in traditional language might be called kingdom theology: theology for the post-ecclesiastical and post-dogmatic era. Whereas ecclesiastical theology is traditionalist and tries to bind people to the past, kingdom theology is about the task of creating 'a new heaven and a new earth' – that is, new people and a new human life-world. In the new millennium this remaking of everything is going to take place in any case. It is already under way, and those of us who think that theology is still important want to see imaginative utopian religious thought helping to shape the human future.

11

Making the Best of It

You are, pronounced a friend on a public occasion, your own worst enemy. He meant that in making out my case I seem unfailingly to choose arguments and forms of words that invite misunderstanding and hostility. Somehow, I can't help being provocative.

It has probably happened on this occasion, too. For I have been developing an argument about a whole series of structural resemblances between two distinct worlds, the world of our postmodernity and the traditional ideal world-at-the-end-of-the-world that religion has called the kingdom of God, Sion, or the New Jerusalem. In both worlds, it seems that:

1. The divine becomes completely immanent, disappearing into a general 'life' or light of intelligibility that pervades everything.
2. The sacred-profane distinction disappears, and organized religion fades away. There is no temple in the New Jerusalem.
3. The world becomes globalized, multi-ethnic, and even 'pentecostal'.
4. The world becomes just the human life-world, fully humanized, and with the old fearsome threatening non-human realm of **It-All** permanently held at bay and even chained up. Life is no longer completely dominated by work.
5. The world, the human life-world, develops a super-intense communicative symbolic life: the world is all 'web', 'media', 'expression'.
6. Everything comes out into the open. Everything becomes public and lit up, and nothing remains dark, deep or hidden.

7. This world becomes the last world, for there is no further world beyond it to be aspired after.

8. Because this world, the human life-world, has become completely illuminated and unmysterious, the human realm is now almost completely free *vis-à-vis* its ancient foes. People become reflexively very highly conscious, and concerned full-time with musical and other forms of symbolic expression. Life becomes performance-art.

In our postmodernity, it seems, there has already occurred a rather extensive 'realization' of Christian eschatology. By which I mean that a lot of things that people used to believe would happen only at the end of the world have recently happened amongst us. And I have tried to demonstrate all this from the idiomatic of ordinary language.

The parallels between our postmodernity and heaven are sometimes comically close. Thus in Greco-Roman mythology there was a traditional food of the goods, *ambrosia*, and drink of the gods, *nectar*; and the words are still familiar, the first in connection with a rice pudding and the second as describing an Australian lager beer. Indeed, the tendency to invoke religious imagery to describe delicious food and drink remains very strong. Again, I commented on the rather quaint Christian iconography of heaven as a world of thirty-three-year-old perfect clones (p.6); and I also commented on the indications that postmodern parents who can call upon the aid of cosmetic surgery and genetic engineering may well opt for children who conform to just such a standard: everybody's sons and daughters will look like the cast of *Baywatch* (p.87).

I am *not*, however, suggesting that there is a hidden hand that directs the course of history. To say that would be to return to the 'dispensationalist' thinking of the past, something that I have certainly no wish to do. What we are seeing is rather the working out within history of Christianity's own inner logic. We have laboured to bring about the kind of world that it taught us to hope for, and we have had some success.

Here I am referring to a whole cluster of eschatological ideas that perhaps originated in ancient Persia and subsequently entered not only into Christianity but also into Judaism, Islam and several other smaller, related faiths. These ideas have had enormous influence historically because they have so deeply affected humanity's *political* hopes, they have deeply affected our *moral* development, and they have affected the way *knowledge* has been developed. We have naturally striven to bring about the fulfilment of our own religious hopes, which have thus shaped our history, not in any supernatural way, but purely immanently. And the process has come to a sort of culmination in our own postmodernity – even, you may think, in our own millennialism in this year of grace 2000.

During the 1980s I tried to put forward a non-realist philosophy of religion, arguing that we should see a religious belief system not as describing how things are in a supernatural realm above us, but as directing us in symbolic language to try to create a particular kind of world. If that is so, then we can sensibly appraise religions in terms of the social worlds they have built: there is a Muslim world, a Hindu world and so on. And from this point of view our own late-modern and post-modern world is clearly the child of post-Reformation Christianity. The faith of our forebears turned out to be a self-fulfilling prophecy, and we have inherited the result.

I have tried to show something of all this happening, in our own time and in our own language; and I know what will be said. I'm being naively utopian about the excesses of our late-capitalism and our consumerism. I'm denying (or at least playing down) the manifest evils and injustices that are everywhere as rampant as ever. My postmodern solar ethic of free self-expression runs into acute difficulties when different cultural groups, each seeking to affirm itself and its values, clash head-on. Markets, whether in ideas or values or signs or goods, never get to be so 'free' as to solve by themselves all problems of *power*. On the contrary, markets will be manipulated by various power-interests unless they are carefully regulated; and the regulators need moral principles to guide them – which surely shows that thoroughgoing market relativism can never by itself be the basis for a social theory. And so on.[1]

I do believe that these objections will be made, and that either they rest upon a misunderstanding, or I have already replied to them. I have been attempting to understand the religious character of our own paradoxical time by looking at ordinary language, and especially at the way it is currently changing. As things turned out, it was through this study of what is currently happening in ordinary language that the detailed analogies between our postmodern world and the Sion of religion have forced themselves upon me. They are *there*, empirically, in the language; and in them we see taking place Christianity's self-transcendence as it moves beyond its old ecclesiastical form into the next, and perhaps final, stage of its development.

Historically we have been hugely influenced by the picture of human life as a pilgrimage through time towards our final home in eternity. A whole series of contrasts was made between the hardships and limitations of our present condition and the ease and glory that awaited the faithful in the heavenly world. Here, all was labour and battle; *there*, all will be rest and songs of triumph. Here, we live in darkness and ignorance; *there*, we will live in the full light of absolute knowledge. Here, inequality and oppression; *there*, unchanging bliss. The ordinary peasant's entire life was spent in unremitting toil and desperate poverty; but in compensation there was Sunday, the day of rest, on which he could contemplate the prospect of a blessed immortality for the obedient faithful.

But suppose that the whole fierce disciplinary ideology *works*, and their efficient toil begins to bring people a measure of prosperity and personal happiness in this present life. They will obviously see in this an immanent realization of their eschatological hopes; and does it not now appear that historical progress towards a purely this-worldly utopia is possible?

Some think so, but others are anxious. Can it last? Will we not soon become soft? We will surely become oddly psychologically divided, if we are to be a disciplined workforce of producers for half the day, and layabout, hedonistic consumers for the other half of the day.

In modern culture people were indeed worried about such

questions; but in postmodernity we are no longer worried, because we do not believe in progress any more, and we are no longer troubled by the old dualistic contrasts between this world and the next, now and then, toil and rest, journey and destination, work and play. The old disciplinary world-view has been so far left behind that we simply no longer think in terms of the basic contrasts that it drew.

I concede that expressions such as **this world** and **this life** do survive in the language. But they are only survivals, because there is no other world and *No Other Life*[2] but this, and in our hearts we know it. In which case the word 'this' is redundant; and we'd do better not to use it, because it tends to bring back with it an old world-picture that we are better off without. In postmodernity the way to religious happiness is by *solar living* – ardently and unreservedly committing oneself to life in all its admitted contingency and transience. Instead of *lifting up* our hearts, we *pour them out*. But we will not be able to do this whole-heartedly so long as the thought lingers that we should perhaps be saving ourselves up for a better life elsewhere.

It is by solar living that we seek to overcome the most glaring paradox of postmodernity. When we are in an 'Enlightenment' mood we may see postmodernity as a condition in which the hopes of the historical period have been partly or largely fulfilled, so that we have reason for celebration. History has reached a certain completion, or at least a plateau of very substantial improvement. But when we are in a more 'Nietzschean' mood we may take a *tragic* view of the postmodern condition. The post-Enlightenment thinker at the end of the line is obliged to refuse all ideas of human progress, embrace tragedy and stare eternal, empty recurrence in the face, for we realize on gaining heaven that life in heaven is **going nowhere**. So I'm torn, you're torn, we're *all* torn between a highly optimistic and a darkly pessimistic view of the postmodern human condition. The sort of person who says that the cup's half-*full* will point to the fulfilment of many of humankind's historical hopes; the sort of person who sees the cup as half-*empty* will say, What have we now got left to hope for? – Nothing.

Nietzsche offers a crumb of comfort when he says that the tragic vision should be seen as a 'tonic' to clear our heads of all the illusions of metaphysics. More substantially, I hope that we can learn by solar living to say an all-out and joyful Yes to life while life lasts. All this is all there is, and all this is purely contingent. But while we have it, we should **make the most of it.**

In postmodernity true religion must start from thoroughgoing philosophical naturalism. But many people will find the point easier to grasp if it is put in theological terms: this is the world at the end of the world, the world that has no beyond, the *last* world. There is no better world beyond this one, no other order of things elsewhere to be aspired after. So there is nothing left for religion to be except a complete and whole-hearted commitment to this world which is the last world. Of course it is not without evil and suffering, but it is all we've got, it is all ours and it is all there is: so we must **make the best of it.** Got that?

Appendix One

Ecclesiastical Theology and Kingdom Theology

Christianity is a faith-tradition which has a particularly complex, though now largely forgotten, logical structure. The official ecclesiastical theology, formulated by the hierarchy in patristic times and still in place today, is relatively well known. What is less well understood is the role in the tradition of kingdom theology, as a vehicle of protest against ecclesiastical theology, as its compensatory counterpart and necessary other, as its forerunner and its promised successor. The hierarchy, who are the chief beneficiaries of ecclesiastical theology, usually disparage kingdom theology and would rather like to be able to bury it altogether – but they can't. It is older than their religion, being deeply rooted in the Bible and the teaching of Jesus; and it will succeed their religion, as they know. The best they have been able to do is kick it upstairs, postponing its realization to the heavenly world on the far side of death. It is 'not immanently realizable', as the correct jargon goes; it is 'not practical politics', as English speakers are apt to say. They may pray 'Thy kingdom come on earth', but they are not looking for a speedy answer to their prayer. Thus the hierarchy and their supporters keep kingdom theology in a state of permanent postponement. After death, maybe; but not on this earth, not within the historical order, not in this life. But they can't deny its authority altogether, and in a most remarkable fashion kingdom theology has survived and has returned to inspire every heretical and utopian movement of renewal and reform. Kingdom theology, like it or not, has always been ecclesiastical theology's bad conscience and better half.

It is a familiar principle of mythological thinking that it seeks to explain and in some measure to reconcile us to some unsatisfactory feature of life, by saying that once upon a time things were otherwise, but some kind of fall or misfortune has occurred to create our present situation.

Thus we may ask, Why is it that unlike snakes, which are able regularly to change their skins and renew their youth, we human beings must become wrinklies and die? Around the world a remarkable range of myths reply that originally human beings were indeed intended to be immortal, but through some kind of negligence or disobedience on the part of the primal human couple the snake was allowed to cheat us of the secret of perpetual youth. The story confirms our feeling that death is a great misfortune, and tells us how we lost our original exemption from it. But this is comforting, because the knowledge that we were at first destined for immortality opens the possibility that we might one day be able to regain it.

Similarly, we may ask, Why are the sexes unequal, and how it is that the men own all the livestock? The Masai answer that originally the sexes were equal and the women had livestock of their own. But they were lazy and didn't get up early enough to take their stock out to pasture. Impatient, the stock escaped to become the wild animals that we see today. Left with no wealth of their own, the women were obliged to marry men and look after *their* stock for them; and so it is to this day. This too is a comforting myth, because it confirms our hunch that the inequality of the sexes in human beings is puzzling and unsatisfactory. If indeed it is not original but arose only through some secondary contingency, then it may perhaps one day be overcome.

In a rather similar way, kingdom theology has always functioned as a compensatory myth within the Christian tradition, the big issue being inequality. To an astounding degree, ecclesiastical theology is an ideology of extreme, cosmic inequality; but kingdom theology says that it doesn't have to be like this. Once there was an ideal condition of 'primitive communism', and we hope that at the end of history it will be restored. Within the present historical order almost all the really significant relationships are profoundly unequal – king and subject, master and servant, man and wife, parent and child – and the greatest inequality of all is the *infinite* inequality between the human self and God, an inequality so great as to make God incomprehensible and leave us capable of relating ourselves to him only indirectly, *via* the apparatus of the mediated, ecclesiastical kind of religion. Our dependence upon mediated religion leaves us in a situation of seemingly permanent subjection to the higher clergy, who control all its apparatus and historically have seldom hesitated to use their power in their own interest: and we are left also in a condition of permanent religious dissatisfaction. But kingdom theology keeps alive the idea that something much better was promised – and even briefly actualized – at the beginning, and will be regained at the end. In kingdom theology religious life becomes immediate. The divine is no longer objectified into an all-powerful cosmic King and Judge, but instead is completely dispersed into people; and with that all lesser inequalities also disappear, allowing the fellowship of persons to become completely reconciled and easy.

To use a jargon once popular amongst New Testament scholars, *in ecclesiastical theology, eschatology is futuristic*, in that the promised time of religious fulfilment is deferred into the far future, and perhaps beyond time altogether and into the next world; whereas *in kingdom theology, eschatology is realized* in the here and now. Thus Jesus lives, and is in his own person, the realization of eschatology: he experiences climactic 'suprahistorical' moments of joyful affirmation, as when he declares, 'I saw Satan fall like lightning from Heaven',[1] even though of course he still lives amongst men and remains vulnerable to conflict, evil and suffering.

It is worth adding that similar themes are found in other religious traditions. The first followers of the Buddha are a brotherhood of equals, and the Buddha himself experiences Nirvana; and similarly the earliest Muslim community was also an ideal brotherhood, while Muhammad himself is thought of as also having had an anticipatory experience of the heavenly world.

Here then is a brief checklist of the principal points of difference between ecclesiastical theology and kingdom theology. *First*, in ecclesiastical theology the whole world of the here and now is subordinated to a greater and better world beyond, whereas in kingdom theology there is no beyond at all. All is arrival, victory, and rest in the here and now.

Most of the other contrasts are related to this first one. Thus, and *secondly*, in ecclesiastical religion God is transcendent, other, and unknown, whereas in kingdom religion God is wholly immanent. *Thirdly*, ecclesiastical religion is mediated by authoritative scriptures, creeds, rituals and priests, whereas kingdom religion is immediate and intuitive. *Fourthly*, in ecclesiastical religion credal, dogmatic faith is a *sine qua non*, whereas kingdom religion is visionary and beliefless. There being no unseen beyond, dogmatic faith is not needed. The reason why one lives *after belief* is the same as the reason why one lives *after history*: one is no longer aspiring after or waiting for anything unseen that one does not already have. *Fifthly*, in ecclesiastical theology there is much emphasis upon rank, hierarchy and inequalities, whereas kingdom theology is highly egalitarian and knows nothing of titles or degrees of rank. Ecclesiastical theology is popish, and kingdom theology is quakerish. *Sixthly*, ecclesiastical theology canonizes one particular vocabulary, a particular cultural tradition and particular lineages of teaching authority, whereas kingdom theology has forgotten tradition and is at last fully 'ecumenical' or globalized – i.e., catholic or pan-ethnic.

Generalizing, and *seventhly*, one may say that in the ecclesiastical world great importance is attached to the fact that much is mysterious, dark, latent, deferred, unseen and generally beyond our ken, whereas in the kingdom everything is explicit, out in the open, equally lit and plain, with no darkness or shadows at all. People are entirely transparent to each other. So also, and *eighthly*, whereas the ecclesiastical world is a world of many languages, of pluralism and discord, the kingdom world is a world of one equal music. And *finally*, in ecclesiastical culture a clear and very important distinction is made between the sacred and profane realms, whereas in the kingdom the sacred/profane distinction is simply not made. Or we may say if we wish that the common speech of plain people is itself the only sacred language.

A corollary of kingdom theology's eschewal of the sacred/profane distinction is that it does not need and does not make the traditional distinction between church and state. The religious community, insofar as it exists at all as a distinct body, is described simply as a society of friends.

Something needs to be added about the sources for kingdom theology. They are principally to be found in the various passages describing an ideal future condition of the world that are to be found almost throughout the Bible, and especially in the prophetic books of the Old Testament, in the teaching of Jesus in the Synoptic Gospels, and in the apocalyptic literature. Theologians studying this material have usually concentrated upon the themes of the visible establishment of God's universal sovereignty and the fulfilment of messianic prophecies, but my interest is in what kingdom theology says about how the religious situation and the social relations of human beings might be different. These latter questions were explored experimentally and on a large scale by the Radical Reformation, from Thomas Munzer in the 1520s to the Putney debates of November 1647, and beyond. In the democratic revolutions of the late eighteenth century and in the philosophy of Kant and Hegel one can see kingdom theology being both normalized and secularized – with unhappy results, for today's secular post-modernity does not understand its own religious roots, and today's church is estranged from its own better half and no longer knows how to reform itself, or even why it needs to do so.

In the prophetic books of the Old Testament, it turns out that Isaiah is the richest in kingdom theology passages. See for example 2.1–4; 9.2–7; 11–12; 25.6–9; 32.14–18; 35; 42.1–9; 49.1–23; 54.1–14 and 60–65 *passim*. But there is vital additional material in Jeremiah 3.15–18; 30.18–31.39, in Ezekiel 36.22–37.28, and in Joel 2.18–29 (with Numbers 11.29), Micah

4.1–7, Zephaniah 3.8–20 and Zechariah 8. These passages helped to make our world, not because God guided the course of history towards the fulfilment of prophecies that he had himself originally inspired, but because *we* laboured to bring about the sort of world that our religion taught us to hope for.

For kingdom theology in the teaching of Jesus – which means, in the Gospels of Matthew, Mark and Luke – it is sufficient to start with one of the many reliable expositions by a Jewish scholar. Geza Vermes, *The Religion of Jesus the Jew* (SCM Press 1993) will serve very well. But Vermes doesn't quite dot the *i*s and cross the *t*s, and therefore doesn't quite get the connection between radical democracy and total divine immanence. See, for example, his treatment of the parable of the sheep and the goats (Matthew 25.31–46). The king says:

> I was hungry and you gave me food,
> I was thirsty and you gave me drink,
> I was a stranger and you welcomed me,
> I was naked and you clothed me,
> I was sick and you visited me,
> I was in prison and you came to me.

Quoting this passage (204f.), Vermes says that 'the prize of salvation is awarded to those who have acted with generosity towards a God in disguise'. But that is insufficient. Jesus really did *equate* religion with humanitarian ethics, and 'faith in God' with performance of the traditional 'works of mercy'. He does *not* say that the 'little one', the poor person who can never repay you for your generosity, is really someone else in disguise. He was a radical.

Appendix Two

Inequalities[1]

In the traditional thinking that prevailed until only yesterday, reality at every level was understood as being created and maintained by a primal, omnipresent and radically unequal relationship. To take the simplest example first, even where the king has not been seen around for some time, everyone still finds it natural to suppose that his kingdom must be held together by the common subjection of every part of it and every person within it to the monarch. That is how the child in its fairy tales assumes reality must be. That is the arrangement that seems to make sense. In the state, in the family and in the universe, there has to be someone wearing the trousers, all the time. The presumption is that even if just at present he happens to be invisible, nevertheless he must still be about somewhere, watching over things, seeing that everything runs as it should and making small corrections as necessary.

The counterpart in philosophy of this idea of a hidden omnipresent ruling power is the ideal, intelligible order, the world of form, the world of theory and of governing rules and standards. Behind the transient particular stands the timeless unified system of rational principles and essences that makes it possible, that conditions it and explains it. Much as before, the plural and ever-changing world of phenomena is held together by the ubiquitous relation of every bit of it to the one ideal controlling order. Just like our traditional religion, science, and fairy tales, philosophy still betrays the influence of the notion that monarchy is the best model for understanding and explaining any ordered system. The system is produced by the ubiquitous action of a ruling principle throughout a domain. So we need everywhere to distinguish between rule and instance, form and matter. If the culture is successfully to establish a universe for us to live in, it has got to bang on relentlessly about a certain ubiquitous distance, dissimilarity and inequality that impinges upon everything. Everywhere there is something primary: it is a general and unchanging intelligible rule, shape or principle. Let's call it a Form. And there is also something secondary: it is a fleeting unstable material appearance or seeming that needs to be shaped and mastered. We've got to have a world, and to make a world for us the culture has got to set up these two themes in complementary apposition. One of them is an active exertion of power, and the other is a passive reception of its impress. Culture must enforce the qualitative difference between these two, and it has also got to permutate them. That is, the manner in which the ruler bears upon the ruled must be varied so as to produce physics, ethics, the social sciences and so on. This in turn means that there must also be correspondingly varied social embodiments of it in human relationships.

So it comes about that the gulf, the omnipresent radical inequality and qualitative difference that makes the world, is variously reflected in society as the gulf between man and woman, between parent and child, king and subject, claimant and official, employer and worker and so forth. To maximize its productive and creative potential, the unequal relationship must be stretched to the greatest cosmic distance, permutated through various modes, and diversely embodied in human social relationships. It is very notable that the most important, symbolically-productive and society-building human ties are precisely the most unequal, those in which the greatest power is wielded. With a certain brutal realism, society has decided that mere friendship is inconsequential. To produce *reality* there must be inequality and the exercise of power.

The unequal universe reaches its logical conclusion and culmination in monotheism. God is an all-powerful Father, one who is of the older generation. Belief in him is right and proper because it comes to us, as *he* comes, from tradition, that is, from the past. The world where he dwells, the exalted, shining, incorruptible world from which we derive all our standards, and by contrast with which the present age here below is always and everywhere seen as a period of decline, somehow contrives to be a primitive golden age set in the past as well as being a golden world above that awaits us after death. Such is the interesting and curious vagueness of religious thought that the strangely blurred location of the golden world – its being linked with the past and tradition, with the present and the above *and* with the future beyond death, all at once – does not matter in the least. The heavenly world of tradition could actually be *seen*, for it was visible in stained glass, on the iconostasis and indeed simply in the liturgy in church. You visited the heavenly world every Sunday, joined its worship and conversed with its inhabitants. These glorious denizens of heaven were figures from the past and tradition, who were now up above and whose company was your personal future. No problem. The heavenly world was somewhat like the aboriginal Dreamtime. It was a mythical, magical, immemorial world that pervaded this present world, and you could slip in and out of it at any time. Thirty years ago, I could do it. You lived in this earthly world of ours somehow with the guidance and help of the heavenly world to which you resorted constantly. It needs to be stressed that so potent is the Dreaming that for me the sacred world truly was more vivid and real than the world of sense. And this living-through-a-dream was a thoroughly effective and perfectly functional way to live. I mean, it worked, it really did *work*.

God's authority over this life of ours was the authority of the above over the below, of limitless power over weakness, of tradition and the older generation over the young, and of men over women. By contrast with God's vast age, wisdom and stability, young people are always seen as impetuous and undisciplined. They are violent unstable tearaways who need firm parental control. Woman is, of course, also perceived as inordinate and threatening, but she is treated as being even younger than youth. She is a child. Her weakness is constitutional: it is something like a natural fault for which she is not altogether to blame, so that it should be handled with indulgent but firmly protective kindness. Her misfortune is to be wayward, fickle and easily led. But there is something worse that makes her almost a potential demoness. Her passions are too strong for her, and in many or most cultures it is (or was) seriously believed that if she is fully sexually awakened she seriously threatens the social order. So she has to be protected from herself and kept in perpetual childhood innocence, sheltered from reality. Until the nineteenth century women were minors almost everywhere. They still are, to a considerable extent.

Not surprisingly, the full weight of cultural and religious pressure was brought to bear on those whose double misfortune it was to be both female and young. To this day even in Western countries it is still felt to be appropriate for a woman to be physically smaller and younger than her husband, so that she shall be treated with just a little (but a little is enough in these matters) of teasing and humouring, as if she were a child, a pet or a plaything. It is not at all incompatible with this regime that society should at the same time regard a reduced and damaged psychological state – anxious, hesitant, over-fastidious and abnormally lacking in self-confidence – as being the *normal* female psychology. And I need not add that just as society equates in a woman a particular kind of damage with 'virtue', so, because we are all of us feminine in relation to God, religion equates its own particular kind of psychological damage with piety. Just as in the social sphere the spectre of reckless female lust is used to warn us all to keep women in subjection, so in the religious sphere the doctrine of original sin is used to keep us all in subjection by advising us of the fearful dangers of pride and presumption. Every believer before God ought to behave something like a woman, and the church has a whole array of father-figures to make the point.

In retrospect, the belief that women are more dangerous than men because their fickle passions threaten the very fabric of society is very surprising. It can surely only have been so widely held because the subjection of women was felt to be constitutive of morality itself and of the entire social order, so that the direst warnings were needed to keep it in place and unquestioned.

Religious conservatives today are probably correct in their instinctive conviction that the subjection of women is central to and has been constitutive of the religious and cultural systems that we have inherited from the past. That is why the most orthodox Jews, Christians and Muslims can come to terms with virtually every aspect of ethical and political modernity, except feminism. It and it alone is of the essence. Sexism is constitutive of their whole world-view, and they cannot possibly abandon it. This way of thinking has been compounded by the venerable defence-mechanism that always leads us to blame not our own impulses but whatever tempts us by provoking them. Woman is to blame for being a provocation to man. Thus Judah the Pious, a mystical writer of the Middle Ages, warns us of the way woman tempts the righteous by hanging out her clothing on the washing-line to dry. It is her plain duty *not* to provoke us in this manner. She should be thoroughly secluded, modest, chaste and covered-up, because every bit of her is a snare. Why, even her little finger burns with lust. That there is projection going on here is indicated by the fact that neither Judah the Pious nor any other of a thousand male writers like him could ever dream of reversing the argument and saying to themselves, 'If a woman is indeed such an inordinately lustful creature and quite unable to control herself, then *my* voice, *my* clothing, *my* little finger must be unbearably provocative to her, so surely *I* am the one who should become silent and secluded?'. But nobody ever heard of a man modestly veiling himself in order not to provoke women and lead them into sin. So there must be projection at work here. The psychological mechanism involved can lead to some pretty surprising opinions. When in 1987 we became abruptly aware of the extremity and seeming frequency of the gross and extraordinary sexual abuse of children, I wondered how far the topic had a traceable history in Judeo-Christian culture. I found only one allusion in ancient Jewish literature: fathers were enjoined to safeguard their sons because boys need to be protected from their own desire for strange men. Men, it seems, are never to blame. It is the women and children who provoke them who are at fault.

To a much greater extent than we yet realize, culture has been made possible by the concentration of power, which in turn has been made possible by the creation and idealization of radically unequal relationships – starting with the man-woman relationship. Man and woman, lord and handmaid, are a complete miniature society, indeed a complete miniature universe. And so far woman has borne the main burden of culture. Do we understand that woman paid for God? That is, the objectification of God, his enthronement in all his glory and majesty as the supreme power and principle of all things, is the exact counterpart of the subjection of woman. For there to be the one, there had to be the other. For him to be so powerful, she must be weak. For him to be so holy, she must be ritually unclean. For his creativity to be so absolute, her sexual energy and creativity had to be denied. For him to be so free and lordly, she must be content to be confined and ancillary (literally, 'handmaidenly'). Woman's self-disparagement is the exact correlate of God's self-affirmation. Hence the wry comments that one often hears from women about the lords of creation: they have an idea of the way they were put down in order to make that lordship possible. For the whole system works precisely by putting woman in general and her sexuality in particular at the opposite pole of the universe from God. We all need God so much precisely because he does not need us at all; and the principle applies *especially* to women. Any suggestion that God could need a *female* around him, that he wants a consort, is blasphemous. Symbolically, woman is sex, and God is spiritualised away beyond sexuality. In Islam he is so far spiritualized as to be beyond even fatherhood. Though still masculine in gender, he is now just pure independent power. So if a *woman* is to please a God who has so completely transcended sex, she must do it by denying her own sexuality and bodiliness with all her might and becoming something like an anorexic nun or a virgin mother. She must be utterly non-threatening, with as little self-esteem as possible. His being so high requires her to be that low.

Thus woman has paid the price. We human beings had to build societies and had to gain some sort of control over ourselves and our environment in order to survive. We had to find out what power was and how to concentrate it, so as first to build coherent societies and then to accumulate the technologies and knowledge-systems that would secure our survival. Woman was the first bit of nature man conquered. Man's knowledge, control and possession of woman became the prime metaphor and model first for God's and then for man's knowledge, control and possession of the world, while at the same time woman's relation to man became a paradigm for the general human relation to God.

It follows from all this that historic Christianity, before the rise of humanitarianism, was not chiefly interested either in human emancipation or in the Christianization of human social relationships. So far as its cultural mission was concerned, it was interested almost exclusively in the construction and maintenance of hierarchies of power and control, angelic, imperial and ecclesiastical. Out of unequal relationships, joined up in vertical chains, a church, an empire and a universe could be built. That is why *the religiously-significant human relationships,* from which we draw the special vocabulary of prayer, *are without exception highly unequal.* They are, principally, the relations of lord to servant, king to subject, judge to defendant and father to son. Less common, but also found, are terms such as master and husband. The attributes of God are also set up in polar terms which stress and permutate the power-gap between God and the believer. In the Western vocabulary with which most of us are familiar, the most frequently invoked contrasts are almighty-weak, holy-sinful, immortal-mortal, eternal-temporal, heavenly-earthly, unchanging-changing and unfailing-frequently failing. The aim of the language in every detail is first to spiritualize power by veiling the primitive sexual violence from which it starts, and then to concentrate and objectify it in God. Civilization is thus made possible, as authority and legitimacy flow down from God through Christ to the twin, complementary hierarchies of church and state. We scarcely need to remind ourselves of the extent to which the architecture, the dress, the iconography, the organization and the liturgy of the

Latin church were derived directly from the later Roman empire in general and from the emperor cult in particular. Though at the personal level classical Christianity was perceived as being about the purification of the self in preparation for the next life, in political terms it was about inequality and power. Where you have any unequal human relationship you have already a *micro-concentration* of power, the power for example of a father over his child or of a man over his wife. Religion picks up such relationships, joins them up in ascending chains, spiritualizes them, and so creates ever-greater and more awesome concentrations of power.

This discussion has now given us a way of formulating the contrast between classical Christianity and the modern religion that has been developing since the Enlightenment. Classical Christianity was about power. It regarded inequality of power in human relationships as a positively good thing, a religiously significant thing, and indeed as providing it with the raw material out of which it could build its world. By contrast, modern Christianity is humanitarian. It is interested in rights, that is, in finding ways of helping, strengthening and revaluing all those who are in various ways at a disadvantage. It doesn't reject power, but it does want to see power more evenly distributed and circulating more freely. It wants to disperse established concentrations of power such as God, the self, the political 'superpowers' and the church hierarchies. It wants a more fluid, decentred and mobile world, in which power and creativity are not fixed in certain hierarchies but instead flow freely, available to all. Where classical Christianity found inequality and ordered gradations of power exciting, we need to be developing a religion that finds equality and spontaneity exciting.

To some extent this is already happening. Modern Christianity has started to get interested in human rights, in social ethics, in the Christianization of secular human relationships, in striving to better the conditions of life of the poorest, and so on. Fine – but completely at variance with the theology and the structures inherited from the past. It is utterly unthinkable that there should be any appeal against the decrees of Calvin's God, or any place for the idea of human rights in his system. Roman Catholic canon law and church structures make Stalinism seem positively liberal. It is preposterous that our daily practices in prayer and worship should so flagrantly contradict the concern for human dignity and freedom that church leaders sincerely profess when they get on their hind legs in public. The fact is that if modern humanitarian Christianity is ever to become established and to assert itself consistently, then it must sooner or later purge itself of cosmic feudalism. Although it has become very ramshackle, the old feudalism still dominates theology, worship, prayer and patterns of organization. People excuse it by saying that because it is all now so ramshackle it doesn't actually do much harm any more; but that is a mistake, like the mistake of supposing that because the British monarchy has not got much political clout any longer it cannot be doing any harm. On the contrary, in the postmodern world, which is so largely made of signs, what really counts is how large you bulk on the mediascape – and *there* the royal family are bigger than ever, not just in Britain but around much of the world. By the same token a good many now-obsolete and noxious religious ideas, rituals and institutions continue to have considerable imaginative and symbolic power, the power that really counts now. They should be purged. If we are sincerely committed to the new more humane and this-worldly kind of Christianity, then of course we must try to expel these relics of a very ugly past.

Easier said than done, no doubt. What is called for is a religion fully committed to the here and now. A religion that, amazingly, finds equality and not inequality sexy. A religion that doesn't inhabit a fantasy-world but whose domain coincides with the only world there is, namely the here-and-now world of signs, the world of communication. This then means dispersing God into people, people into their own communicative activities, and the cosmos into an unceasing, endlessly self-renewing process of communal artistic production. *Our* work of art.

Religion in that world will be a way of celebrating a human emancipation that is continually to be striven for and realized afresh. For the Christianized version of a postmodern world that I am describing cannot be suddenly realized once and for all and then fixed as a permanent achievement. Rather, it has itself to be a continuous productive activity, which is why there needs to be a continual re-enactment of the liturgy (*leitourgia*, public service) of religion.

We will picture a postmodern eucharist as a ceremonial enactment of the death and dispersal of God. God goes out into language, that is, into humanity. He passes out into multiplicity and, dying, communicates his power and creativity to us. Thus the law comes to an end and gospel takes its place, for by 'the law' I just mean the hierarchized disciplinary universe that people inhabited during the entire historical period, and which has so recently come to an end. Yes, we certainly recycle the past, but we do so ironically; yes, we love nostalgia and revivals, but our very ability to revive all earlier periods, we now see, shows that we are no longer locked into a period that is specifically our own in the way everyone used to be. Not locked into one period, being now too ironical and pluralistic for that, we cannot now be *held* so rigorously by the law as people once were. We know there are many alternatives, so we know that those other possibilities are options open to us. So we come to the knowledge that *we* made all those other options, and now it is only a matter of time before we grasp that we also made the law itself and it too is optional. And now we are free from the law, because it has ceased to be absolute. Everything is permitted – including even an optional, ironical return to the Law – and nothing is objectively obligatory.

We are free because we are not constrained by period, by history, and by the law in the way we were. In the ancient cyclical and dispensational systems world history passed through a series of theologically-qualified epochs. What you could do and become was circumscribed by the theological character of the particular era into which you had been born.

But our postmodern age is Christian and eschatological in that we find ourselves living in a strange open-textured period after the end of period, after history and the law, and therefore after the death of the old Almighty One who formerly concentrated and absorbed all power into himself. The huge diffusion of information this century has made us all so pluralistic, so knowing, so ironical that everything has been dispersed, even God. God has brought history to an end by dying, by giving himself to us, returning his power of defining reality into *us*. So we are no longer within a period whose theological character has been antecedently defined for us by him. Or rather, the special theological character of the present age is its *absence* of any impressed theological character. This freedom, this openness and *lack of any destiny* which has resulted from God's own voluntary self-dispersal marks our own queer post-'period' period as the first truly *Christian* period. We are emancipated because we are not stuck with any ready-made destiny. We are not on rails of any kind. All the *grands récits*, the great narratives, have passed away. Our future is open. It is for us to make. This is the real age of grace, after history. And it is what our eucharist must celebrate.

Notes

1. *Sheer Bliss*

1. Germaine Bazin, *Paradeisos: The Art of the Garden*, London: Cassell 1990.

2. E.g. Genesis 7.11, 8.2.

3. E.g. Genesis 8.21.

4. Mircea Eliade, *From Primitives to Zen: A Thematic Sourcebook of the History of Religions*, London: Collins 1979, ch.II, nos. 44, 46, pp.83, 85.

5. The changes I am describing here were first described in various American books of popular sociology, such as David Riesman, *The Lonely Crowd*, New York: Anchor Books, 1950, 315ff. and Erving Goffman, *The Presentation of Self in Everyday Life*, New York: Anchor Books 1959.

6. The obsolescence of these words was reported years ago by G. E. M. Anscombe in a famous article, 'Modern Moral Philosophy', in *Philosophy*, Volume 33.

7. The title of a novel by Kingsley Amis (1968).

8. A false antithesis, as Aristotle insists.

2. *Different Perceptions*

1. One of the first writers to introduce this vocabulary was Guy Debord. But he didn't like it as much as I do.

2. *The First and Second Prayer Books of King Edward VI*, ed. E. C. S. Gibson, Everyman's Library, No. 448, London: Dent 1957, 249.

3. E.g., *Understanding Vision*, ed. Glyn W. Humphreys, Readings in Mind and Language, Vol. 1, Oxford: Blackwell 1992.

3. *Get Real!*

1. *Meditations* VI, etc.

2. From Shelley's *A Defence of Poetry*, 1821, echoing (surprisingly) a passage in Samuel Johnson's *Rasselas*, 1759, ch.10: the poet must write as 'the legislator of mankind . . . a being superior to time and place'.

3. Compiled from the materials supplied by the Oxford Dictionaries of *English Idioms*, 1993; *Proverbs*, 1992; and the *New Oxford Dictionary of English*, 1998, with some additions of my own. The new post-Hegelian sense of the world as simply the human world is well articulated in a much-quoted line from the young Karl Marx: 'Man is not an abstract being, squatting outside the world. Man is the human world, the state, society.'

4. *The Religious Character of Postmodern Experience*

1. My talk of 'history' as the period during which people groan under the regime of great disciplinary institutions is of course derived from Nietzsche. The ones he has chiefly in mind are pretty much the same as the ones I've groaned under: the state, the church, the army, the university.

2. Consider the abnormality, the extremity, of the historical Vincent van Gogh – and the democratic ordinariness of his huge present-day popularity. A vision that was crazy then is commonplace now.

3. See, for example, Giles Kepel, *The Revenge of God*, Cambridge: Polity Press 1994.

4. See my *The Meaning of It All in Everyday Speech*, London: SCM Press 1999, for language's attempt to keep **it** out.

5. *An Essay in Aid of a Grammar of Assent*, 1870, London and Indiana: University of Notre Dame Press 1979, 98ff. (Part 1, ch.5, 1).

6. Sir Peter Paul Rubens once put in his garden a statue of 'Hermathena', symbolizing the marriage of Art and Commerce. But despite such gestures the whole world of money remains somewhat under a moral cloud in Britain. Why? – because, it seems, money is part of the **it** that threatens the quality of personal intercourse. It needs to be pushed back, and kept out of sight.

7. It is in this quarter that we can find the reason why so many of the 'Catholic novelists' have also been accomplished *comic* novelists. English examples include Waugh, Greene, Spark and Lodge.

8. The word 'mindhold' was coined by G. E. M. Anscombe many years ago, on the analogy of 'foothold'.

5. *Postmodern Religious Belief*

1. John Milbank, *The Word Made Strange: Theology, Language, Culture*, Oxford: Blackwell 1997, 1.

6. *The World at the End of the World*

1. I should confess that 'dystopia' now seems to have replaced 'cacotopia'. For the belief in progress, see John Passmore, *The Perfectibility of Man*, London: Duckworth 1970.

2. Jeremiah 31.33, cited in Hebrews 10.16.

3. As I reported in *The New Religion of Life*, the Fourth Gospel appears to use the word *zoe* in both senses.

4. Revelation 21.22ff.

5. I Corinthians 15.28, AV and RSV. The biblical symbolism is very striking: for notice that when God is localized and objectified, as in the Second Temple, God 'dwells in thick darkness'; but when God is scattered across everything, everything is bright, and there is no darkness at all. The more God is objectified, the less God can be known.

6. Revelation 21.25. As Christianity lapsed back into the old kind of religion, it locked the city gates, and gave the keys to Peter and his successors in office.

7. Ibid.

8. In Britain, the sporting calendar is a highly-developed annual cycle of events which changes little, decade after decade. It is temporal, but it is extra-historical, like the church's liturgical year and the child's year. So, in effect, much of life is extra-historical, anyway – and people *like* it so.

7. *Passing Out*

1. The *OED* entry s.v. is very useful: it appears in volume V of 1901.

2. In early Christianity, if you were really serious about religion, you fled 'the world' (i.e., your neighbour). A 'monk' is literally a person who lives alone.

3. Michel Foucault, *Histoire de la Folie*, 1961, ET *Madness and Civilization*, London: Tavistock Publications, 1967, ch.2.

4. See R. W. Southern, *The Making of the Middle Ages*, London: Hutchison 1953, Plate I: the Crucifixion, from the Gospels of Countess Judith, c.1051–1065 (now in the Pierpont Morgan Library, New York, MS 709).

It is worth remarking that the contorted figure of the Crucified has a prehistory in Byzantine art, before its sudden appearance and great popularity in the West. But in Byzantine treatments of a major sacred scene, notice that the various people present are not all looking at each other in an organized way. Rather, they react as individuals or in little groups of two or three, expressing awe, joy or grief. Contrast Giotto, in whom the same scene is made into an organized drama by a complex network of eye-contacts. In Giotto, the sacred is not just other, revealing itself and attracting individual responses: no, it is fully brought down into a complex network of human interactions. The Sacred shows itself in and through the dramatics of human social life – a uniquely Western religious insight and achievement, and one that arguably makes Giotto the first great Christian humanist.

5. Bernard McGinn, *The Growth of Mysticism: From Gregory the Great to the Twelfth Century, The Presence of God: A History of Western Christian Mysticism*, Vol. II, London: SCM Press 1995, 309–23.

6. The emphasis upon the naked suffering body in Christianity has been so strong that the writer Gore Vidal has dismissed it as 'a sado-masochistic religion'. I retort that if we are to understand the origins of Western humanitarianism we must disdain that charge.

7. Because Jewish and Christian thought are so closely interwoven it is arguable that some Jews do see Judaism as also completing its historical mission by transcending itself into universal religious humanism.

8. *Is Anything Still Sacred?*

1. Emile Durkheim, *The Elementary Forms of the Religious Life*, ET by J. W. Swain, London: Allen and Unwin 1915, 37, 47.

2. Mircea Eliade, *A History of Religious Ideas*, Vol. 1, ET by W. R. Trask, London: Collins 1979, xvi. Unfortunately, Eliade did not live to complete the work, which in its truncated form ends just as modernity is beginning.

3. *The New Oxford Dictionary of English*, 1998, svv. numen, numinous.

4. Revelation 1.17; compare Daniel 8.17. Throughout the Bible, direct contact with the sacred is liable to cause death: Numbers 4.15.

5. Delivered on his behalf by Harold Pinter, Granta Publications 1990, and published without any of the normal details through which a target might be identified.

6. P.4.

7. P.7.

8. P.16.

9. Published in *Trois Contes* (1877).

9. *Postmodern Saints: The Selfless Professional and the Solar Performer*

1. Cambridge undergraduate slang for a natural scientist.

2. See my *Solar Ethics*, SCM Press 1995. Notice that long hair is associated with expressionism or 'solarity', and that the sun, symbolically, is pictured as long-haired.

3. Especially I Corinthians 4.9f.; Hebrews 10.33.

4. E.g., Matthew 10.26f.; Mark 4.22; Luke 8.16f.; Ephesians 5.11–14. The end-time is always associated with the triumph of light over darkness, and of exposure over concealment.

5. See *The Ecstasy of Communication* (*L'Autre par lui-même*, 1987); ET, New York: Semiotext(e), 1988, 21ff.

6. We should note, however, that some good artists like Jackson Pollock cannot bear publicity, and others such as B. Traven, J. D. Salinger and Thomas Pynchon have chosen to make a counter-cultural statement by deliberately shunning publicity. I note that all these four persons are Americans: perhaps it is in America that media hype is most destructive to artists and to art.

11. Making the Best of It

1. I anticipated some of these ideas and criticisms in *The Time Being*, SCM Press 1992, especially in Chapter 5(v), 72–82.

2. The title of, and the key phrase in, a novel by Brian Moore (1993).

Appendix One: Ecclesiastical Theology and Kingdom Theology

1. Luke 10.18.

Appendix Two: Inequalities

1. This piece is a Sea of Faith Conference Lecture from 1988 and hitherto unpublished, though some of the ideas in it and some phrases subsequently went into *Radicals and the Future of the Church*, 1989. My argument is indebted to Fatna A. Sabbah's very fine *Woman in the Muslim Unconscious*, Pergamon Press 1984. A. O. Lovejoy's celebrated book *the Great Chain of Being*, Harvard 1936, made familiar the idea that in the old hierarchical world-pictures difference of rank is the basic brick that is used for building the world. But Lovejoy did not develop the political implications of his theme as he might have done.

Index